Edison Branch Library
18400 Joy Rd.
Detroit, MI 48228
(313) 852-4515

The People of Clarendon County

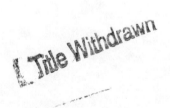

MAR '08

Detroit, MI 48228
(313) 852-4515

The People of Clarendon County
A Play by Ossie Davis

with

Photographs and Historical Documents,
and Essays on the Education That Can End Racism

Edited by
Alice Bernstein

Third World Press
Chicago

Third World Press
Publishers since 1967
Chicago

© 2007 by Alice Bernstein
"The People of Clarendon County" © 2005 by the Estate of Ossie Davis

All rights reserved. No part of the material protected by this copyright notice
may be reproduced, stored in a retrieval system, or transmitted in any form
by any means, electronic mechanical, photocopying, recording or otherwise
without prior written permission, except in the case of brief quotations
embodied in critical articles and reviews. Queries should be addressed to
Third World Press, P.O. Box 19730, Chicago, IL 60619.

First Edition
Printed in the United States of America

Cover design by Keir Thirus
Layout and interior design by Jan M. Wagner

Library of Congress Control Number: 2007906728
ISBN-10 0-88378-287-1
ISBN-13 978-0-88378-287-3

12 11 10 09 08 07   6 5 4 3 2 1

ACKNOWLEDGMENTS

Many people had to do with the coming-to-be of this book and I welcome the opportunity to acknowledge them here. I am profoundly grateful to Ossie Davis for entrusting me with the publication of his play in which history, drama, activism for justice, and a large feeling for people come together. His enthusiasm about my vision of having *The People of Clarendon County* alive in a new way and in relation to Aesthetic Realism, the education that can end racism, inspired me. I cherish our conversations. And I am enormously grateful to Ruby Dee for warmly supporting this book; and to Nora Davis Day, literary agent Susan Crawford, and the staff of Emmalyn Productions—notably Arminda Thomas and Latifah Martin—for their assistance, including photographic resources from the Dee and Davis Archive.

I also gratefully acknowledge the First Amendment Center for permission to publish remarks by Ossie Davis from the "Speaking Freely" PBS television program, which aired in 2000; William Morrow & Company for permission to quote from *With Ossie & Ruby: In This Life Together*, by Ossie Davis and Ruby Dee, (2000); Cornell University Press for permission to quote from *Not for Bread Alone: A Memoir*, by Moe Foner and Dan North, with Foreword by Ossie Davis (Copyright 2002 by Cornell University); the Aesthetic Realism Foundation, for permission to reprint the essay by Barbara McClung under the title "A Science Class Combats Prejudice" from *The Right of Aesthetic Realism to Be Known* (issue #1201, Copyright 1996); and for permission to reprint portions of "Racism Can End" by Ellen Reiss (issue #1264, Copyright 1997). I am also grateful to Ms. Reiss for her discussion of the Ossie Davis play and permission to quote from it.

The generosity of Joseph A. DeLaine, Jr., who preserved so much history and made available to me his family archives on the Clarendon County parents and children, is a cause of large gratitude. And I am indebted to Dr. Julie Magruder Lochbaum of Truman State University for writing the first biography of Rev. DeLaine, *The Word Made Flesh*, and for guiding my historic research.

I thank Jack Humphery, editor of the *South Carolina Black News*, whose support for my work all these years had much to do with the coming-to-be of this book; Dr. Tom Hanchett, historian with the Levine Museum of the New South (Charlotte, NC), for providing historical perspective on school desegregation in South Carolina; and Alan Ross, Esq. for researching documents in relation to the career of Judge J. Waties Waring.

Conversations with Karen Van Outryve, Anne Fielding and Barbara Allen, consultants on the faculty of the Aesthetic Realism Foundation, and with Margot Carpenter, the Executive Director, were important to the development of this book, for which I thank them.

I am deeply grateful to Ellen Reiss, Class Chairman of Aesthetic Realism, for her scholarship, good will, and love for exactitude. Her kind interest in the people, history, and events told of here, and her immense encouragement to have my thoughts and writing about them be as good and useful as possible, were crucial to this book.

I happily thank my husband, David Bernstein, for believing in me and encouraging every aspect of my work, which is so much a part of our lives.

And, of course, my gratitude is immeasurable—as all humanity's will be—to Eli Siegel, founder of the philosophy Aesthetic Realism, for the knowledge that can end racism.

Any errors of content or form in this book are my responsibility alone.

CONTENTS

Note: In various documents DeLaine is spelled in different ways. Here we use the prevalent spelling of DeLaine, while noting that the family's preference is for De Laine. For the lawsuit Briggs v. Elliott, *we use Elliott and not Elliot as it sometimes appears in print.*

The use of the words "Negro" and "colored" in the 1940s-1960s to refer to African Americans, has been retained in the original sources.

INTRODUCTION

Our idea of getting an education did not come out of wanting to imitate anyone whatever. It grew out of...the desire to know not just a little, but a great deal. We wanted to know how to calculate an eclipse, to know what Hesiod and Livy thought; we wished to know the best thoughts of the best minds that lived with us.

–Fanny Jackson Coppin

Clarendon County is a rural community in South Carolina where the Rev. Joseph Armstrong DeLaine (1898-1974) lived, taught, and preached until 1955. In the 1940s he courageously led his friends and neighbors—black sharecroppers, domestic workers, and laborers—in joining the NAACP, an act which took great courage at that time. In the 1950s he led their fight for better schools for their children, schools "equal" to those of the white residents.

Many parents stood up for the right of their children to be educated. Among them were William and Mary Ragin, and Harry and Eliza Briggs. Harry Briggs had fought in the segregated armed forces during World War II, and is quoted as saying, "I don't guess I spent three years in the United States Navy to keep the world safe for Jim Crow." For the choice they made, each of them faced economic retribution and life-threatening violence.

Not even they, however, dreamed how far their fight would go. Their 1951 lawsuit, *Briggs v. Elliott*, was the first of five cases leading to the breakthrough 1954 Supreme Court Decision *Brown v. Board of Education*. In that famous ruling, the U.S. Supreme Court declared that segregation is unconstitutional and must end "with all deliberate speed."

The following year, the story behind *Briggs v. Elliott* was made into a dramatic sketch by a young actor in New York City named Ossie Davis. *The People of Clarendon County*, his short play, was performed once, in 1955, for an enthusiastic audience of union brothers and sisters at Local 1199 in New York City, known at the time as the Retail Drug Workers Union. The three young actors, whose names would soon be known throughout the world, were Ossie Davis, Ruby Dee, and Sidney Poitier.

Brown v. Board of Education led to a great upheaval in this country about what people deserve and heralded the Civil Rights movement of the 1960s. It wasn't until 2003, however, after I began writing for the *South Carolina Black News*, that I first heard of Rev. DeLaine. My colleague Christopher Balchin, a high school history teacher and Aesthetic Realism Associate, sent me an e-mail containing several stories about him, and I was gripped by what I read. This was the beginning of a remarkable journey during which I met many people with whom I am now friends, and which led to my discovery of the Ossie Davis play.

The People of Clarendon County is a simple play about two of the biggest issues in the world: education and equality. As I'll describe, Ossie Davis wanted me to use his play in behalf of these goals and in relation to the knowledge that can make equality not just a dream, but a vibrant, cherished reality for our children and all people: Aesthetic Realism.

Some Background

Aesthetic Realism is the philosophy founded in 1941 by Eli Siegel (1902–1978), the American poet and educator. I am a journalist whose writing is informed by my study of it. The answer to racism, I have seen, is in this principle, stated by Mr. Siegel: "The resolution of conflict in self is like the making one of opposites in art." The commentary "Racism Can End," by Class Chairman of Aesthetic Realism Ellen Reiss, reprinted here, tells more about this needed education.

Every moment in life presents us with the choice either to know and respect the world and people, or to look on them with contempt. *Contempt*, the "false importance or glory from the lessening of things not oneself," Mr. Siegel described as "the greatest danger or temptation" of humanity. It is as everyday as the sarcasm between husband and wife, a child's sticking out her tongue, or the way we have our own thoughts while pretending we are listening. Contempt is the cause of all human injustice. While it sometimes takes ordinary forms, some of which I've mentioned, it also leads to the greatest horrors. But, contempt can *change* through education, through criticism, when we see how deeply we despise ourselves for having it. That is what happened to me.

As a child growing up in Brooklyn, I had an eager desire for knowledge. But I also hoped to be important by feeling superior to others. This desire made me unkind, including to the people closest to me. In fact, I was prejudiced against my own sister, Judy! Because her appearance and disposition were different from mine—she was blond, lively, and welcoming; I was a brunette, serious, and aloof (I called it being dignified)—I felt she showed me up. So I tried to show *her* up by acting like I was deeper and made of finer stuff. Because she was different, I simply assumed she was against me, and I was often mean to her. I felt awful about my meanness, but I didn't know how to be any other way.

This contemptuous attitude continued with people outside my family. I'm ashamed that I once called a little boy an ugly name because his skin was darker than mine. I still remember his pained face after all these years.

Then, when I was about seven, my parents began studying Aesthetic Realism and our family was fortunate to have lessons with Eli Siegel. We began to learn the large meaning of "relation." At age ten, I brought to one lesson a picture of a Dutch girl dressed in the traditional cap, apron, and wooden shoes. Looking at it, Mr. Siegel said: "She represents you." I was very surprised because we were so different. But then he asked, "Could she feel hemmed in like you?"

"Yes," I answered.

"Has she laughed at any jokes," he asked, "and cried after arguing with her mother?"

As I began to see her feelings were like my own, this little girl, far away, became important to me, close to me, even dear to me. I was learning the way of seeing that makes for real pride, and I began to understand why I felt ashamed when I was unjust to my sister or any other person, including another little girl who spoke with a foreign accent. I was having contempt, and that is not what my mind was meant for.

In Aesthetic Realism lectures I later attended, as I heard Mr. Siegel discuss world thought and history, and the human conflict throughout the centuries between respect and contempt, I came to a wider understanding of what ordinary contempt could lead to. Yes, slavery arose from contempt, as did Nazism in Germany, apartheid in South Africa, and the hideous racial injustices in the United States. I felt then and do even more so now, that when people are clear about the cause, these horrors can really change, really end!

We all want to esteem ourselves, and in *Self and World* (Definition Press, 1981), Mr. Siegel writes about the authentic means of doing so: "There is such a thing as the ethical unconscious. Well, if we praise ourselves and we know we have been unfair to outside reality in doing so, there is a nervous conflict in us.... To love ourselves really we have to love and want to know outside reality; that is, the outside form of ourselves, or the world."

The People of Clarendon County is a drama about people standing up for justice and ethics; opposing a form of contempt that had become institutionalized. Because of their courage and ethical determination, along with that of many others, segregation is illegal today. Yet contempt persists and racism goes on.

Conversations with Ossie Davis— and How This Book Came to Be

In May of 2004, in preparation for an interview with him, I sent Ossie Davis articles I'd written which had appeared in my column in *South Carolina Black News* and elsewhere. These included a story about Reverend DeLaine and my interview with Congressman Elijah Cummings of Maryland, then Chair of the Congressional Black Caucus. In these articles, I wrote about Aesthetic Realism. Knowing that Mr. Davis had studied with Sterling Brown at Howard University, I also sent an account by Leila Rosen, an Aesthetic Realism Associate and high school English teacher, of the 1966 lecture Eli Siegel gave on Sterling Brown. In it, Mr. Siegel placed this little-known African American poet as one of the important writers in American literature.

As Ossie Davis and I spoke in the spring of 2004, various subjects came together. Referring to what I had sent him, Mr. Davis said he was glad that Rev. DeLaine was now getting some deserved recognition. And he was very interested in my recollections of having attended Mr. Siegel's lecture on Sterling Brown.

Our discussion turned to the work I was then doing with my husband, David: visiting elementary schools in New York and Maryland to encourage children to care for books and reading. David and I would speak with the children about sentences like this one, from the chapter "Books" in *Children's Guide to Parents and Other Matters*, by Eli Siegel: "Every time you read a book, someone else's feelings meet yours, and mix with yours." Mr. Davis was affected to hear that in one predominantly African American school, in a discussion with second graders, I had expressed regret that people with skin like mine had been so unjust to people with skin like theirs. And he was very moved as I described how we'd asked a little boy if he thought his feelings could be put into a book and meet someone else's feelings, and how a look of wonder had come to the boy's face.

A few weeks later, the anthology *Aesthetic Realism and the Answer to Racism*, which I edited and co-authored, was published by Orange Angle Press. I believe it was then that Ossie Davis and I exchanged books. He sent me *With Ossie & Ruby: In This Life Together*. It was in this autobiography that I learned of the play *The People of Clarendon County*. After searching unsuccessfully for it, I called to ask Ossie Davis how I could read it. He said that it had never been published and he wasn't sure the manuscript still existed, but that if it did, it would be among the Dee and Davis papers at the Schomburg Center for Research in Black Culture.

On July 20, 2004, he wrote in a letter to me: "[The play] holds a special place in my heart. It marked the beginning of my association with Local 1199, an association that has brought me great satisfaction and joy over the years."

In October, I found the original manuscript at the Schomburg Center, and called Mr. Davis. "I'd better sit down before I fall," he said. I described reading a photocopy of it on the subway, imagining children throughout the country acting it in their schools. "Yes," he said, "yes. So you think there's life in it?"

"I do, very much" I told him. I mentioned my idea of writing an introduction to a performance of the play, which would have what Aesthetic

Realism explains about the cause of and answer to prejudice. I felt this combination could be a powerful means of fighting racism.

"Well, then," Ossie Davis said, "you certainly have my approval. You have my permission without any restrictions, to do what you feel is best."

I also mentioned at that time that I was applying for a fellowship to continue my writing and speaking in new ways. When Mr. Davis heard about this, he immediately offered to write a letter in my behalf, saying "I know about your work and about Aesthetic Realism." I'm grateful he did just that! That letter from November 18, 2004, contains some of his feeling about the coming to be of this book:

> Alice Bernstein has dedicated her life to ending racism in this country…. One of Alice Bernstein's life goals is encouraging young people to read books and enjoy writing. She does this by visiting elementary schools speaking to young people about prejudice— even within herself—and how it can change to kindness…. She also spoke on "Can Racism End? Yes! Aesthetic Realism Shows How" at Thurgood Marshall Academy in Harlem and at Brooklyn College.
>
> Remarkably, Ms. Bernstein has unearthed a play I wrote fifty years ago, "The People of Clarendon County."… [She] is writing an introduction based on what she has learned about people and history from Aesthetic Realism which she has studied for decades.

As our conversation in October 2004 was ending, Mr. Davis added, "When you introduce the play in New York, I would be happy to join you." How I wish that might have been! Ossie Davis died on Friday, February 4, 2005.

I am profoundly grateful to Ruby Dee for embracing this book project and wanting it to succeed. On November 2, 2006, while I was preparing the manuscript, Ms. Dee wrote a letter of recommendation, in which she gives further background about this publication:

> In her commitment to telling the story of the civil rights struggles…Alice uncovered the play, *The People of Clarendon County*. The piece, written in 1955 by my late husband, Ossie Davis, celebrated the Rev. Joseph DeLaine and parents in rural South Carolina who sacrificed so much for their children to get a decent education. Ossie, Sidney Poitier, and I performed the piece for Local 1199's Negro History Week celebration….
>
> Alice was determined that *The People of Clarendon County* should have a wider audience. With Ossie's permission and encouragement, she prepared the play—accompanied by original sources and photographs, as well as her own introduction—for publication. Due to her tireless efforts… [it] will soon arrive at a bookstore near you.
>
> It moved my husband to think that fifty years later, school children might learn about history by reading or acting in his play. In addition, Alice's book will also inform people about the success of the Aesthetic Realism Teaching Method in enabling children to learn every subject, and ending prejudice in the classroom. I look forward to the play's first revival.

Drama, History, and Social Activism

We claim for ourselves every single right that belongs to a freeborn American...and until we get these rights we will never cease to protest and assail the ears of America. The battle we wage is not for ourselves alone but for all true Americans. It is a fight for ideals, lest this, our common fatherland, false to its founding, become in truth the land of the thief and the home of the Slave.

−W.E.B. DuBois

History and drama are deeply intertwined in Ossie Davis's life and career. He and Ruby Dee were close friends of Dr. W.E.B. DuBois. They knew the leaders of the Civil Rights movement and participated in many pivotal events in behalf of labor and social justice in the U.S. and internationally. Mr. Davis delivered eulogies at the funerals of Malcolm X and Dr. Martin Luther King, Jr., and was considered by many to be a central voice of the African American community. His writing contains much about people and events in history, including slavery and Jim Crow. "The aim of history," Eli Siegel wrote in the book *Definitions, and Comment*, "is to make past feeling felt more, or, simply, the past felt more." I believe that was a large aim of Ossie Davis.

In a television interview with Ken Paulson in 2000, Ossie Davis expressed deep feeling about tragic events of fifty years earlier: the lynching of Harry T. Moore in Florida; the deaths of seven boys in Martinsville, Virginia; the lynching of Willie McGee. These names also appear in *The People of Clarendon County*. "As artists and as writers, that's our job," he told the television audience: "to rescue these people from oblivion and invisibility and give them life and form."

He has given "life and form" in notable ways as a writer, for example, in his fine novel for young people, *Just Like Martin*, set in Alabama in 1963; in his plays, including the Broadway success *Purlie Victorious*, a hilarious, biting satire of racism in the Jim Crow South (later made into the musical

Purlie); *Escape to Freedom*, about slavery and the young Frederick Douglass; and *Langston*, about poet Langston Hughes and the Harlem Renaissance. As one of the narrators of the 1994 documentary "The African Burial Ground: An American Discovery," Mr. Davis said of the slaves buried there, "If I had the privilege of asking them, I would ask this question: What did you hope for in all that happened to you?"

Some Key Events Leading to *The People of Clarendon County*

The desire in Ossie Davis and Ruby Dee to join acting and social activism has been passionate throughout their lives, and it flourished in their association with Moe Foner, the Director of the Bread and Roses Cultural Project of Local 1199. Mr. Davis wrote in his Foreword to Mr. Foner's memoir, *Not for Bread Alone* (Cornell University Press, 2002):

> Ruby and I had begun our civil rights activism by acting in a benefit performance of a play called Anna Lucasta in 1946 to raise money for the families of two soldiers killed by the Klan in Monroe, Georgia [George Dorsey and Roger Malcom]. After that...we demonstrated, picketed, and rallied.... It was at Local 1199 under the tutelage of Moe Foner that we finally found the focus and began to fulfill in the deepest, most personal way our commitment to the struggle, rendering our most conspicuous service to the cause.
>
> From the start [Moe] was looking for something more than a mere recitation of poems and speeches from the past. What about the present, he asked me and Ruby, something current, something directly connected to the struggle for civil rights.... Why not an original

piece, I replied, a little drama on what was happening in the daily headlines swirling around us, which we would stage for the membership by standing up and reading into a microphone, living newspaper-style?

The People of Clarendon County was the first result, and as he describes its history, you feel his excitement. In *With Ossie & Ruby*, Mr. Davis writes:

> On May 17, 1954, the Supreme Court handed down one of its most momentous decisions ever, *Brown v. Board of Education*, which outlawed segregation in the public schools.
>
> America, stunned, as after a hurricane, gathered to assess the impact.... I hungrily read it all, hoping to find a centerpiece for our program. I found what I wanted in the people of Clarendon County, South Carolina, and in Reverend Joseph DeLaine, a respected leader in the black community.
>
> Nobody was out to make history, certainly not to change the ways of segregation; but the white parents there had thirty buses to carry their kids to and from school, while the black parents had none.... Several black parents, represented by Thurgood Marshall and the NAACP Legal Defense Fund, sued on the basis that their rights to equal treatment under the Fourteenth Amendment were being denied....
>
> The dramatic sketch that followed almost wrote itself....We called it *The People of Clarendon*

County. The audience in the crowded 1199 union
hall was deeply moved by our presentation. Moe
was so pleased, he not only gave us the fifty
dollars apiece he had promised, but also asked us
to do the same kind of show for the union's next
Negro History Week program.

So began one of the most fruitful and rewarding
associations of our lives.

Sidney Poitier told me with pleasure that he remembered the
performance at the 1199 union auditorium and his playing a father who was
angry about the rundown segregated school. We both remarked on the
significance of the fact that years later he played Thurgood Marshall in the
1991 film *Separate But Equal.* The sketch by Ossie Davis inspired playwright
Loften Mitchell to develop the material into a three-act play with many more
characters, *A Land Beyond the River.* Produced in 1957, it had a run of almost
a year at the Greenwich Mews Theatre in New York City. And Julian Wiles
of Charleston Stage wrote and produced *The Seat of Justice*, about *Briggs v.
Elliott.* It ran in 2004, celebrating the fiftieth anniversary of *Brown.*

While Ossie Davis and Ruby Dee had a long, productive, creative
affiliation with Local 1199, after the performance in 1955, *The People of
Clarendon County* was essentially forgotten. Finding and reading this play
affected me deeply.

Looking at the Play

The only extant version of the script contains crossings out and lists the
characters as NARRATOR, DEE, and POITIER—for the actors who played
them. Sometimes the NARRATOR shifts from Ossie Davis to Rev. DeLaine.
The DEE and POITIER characters are Mary (Mable) and William Ragin,
signers of the original *Briggs* petition. The play script published here contains
the names of the characters—the dramatis personae.

I sent a copy of the script to Ellen Reiss, the Class Chairman of Aesthetic Realism, asking if she would consider discussing it in a class for those who teach Aesthetic Realism and use it professionally. She welcomed my request and on November 23, 2004, she looked at the play in relation to this principle stated by Eli Siegel: "All beauty is a making one of opposites, and the making one of opposites is what we are going after in ourselves."

I'll mention four points in this careful class discussion:

1. Ms. Reiss spoke of how Ossie Davis saw the dramatic art. There was a deep conviction in him, she said, that "if something is going on which people should know about and have feeling about—whatever it is, drama should be able to present it!"

2. She pointed to opposites within this play: the *intimate* and the *wide*, which can take the form of a desire to be comfortable and cozy, and a desire to stand up for justice. The fight between these, she said, is in the play's characters as it is in humanity. And she spoke about the viewpoint of Aesthetic Realism that you cannot *really* have a comfortable life unless you are interested in what other people deserve.

3. Ms. Reiss said, "This play shows what Mr. Siegel explained, that *'ethics is a force'* in history. For example: the fact that a person can have an increasing clearness about what he or she deserves is a huge thing in the history of mind and in the history of people dealing with other people." In the play we see this increasing clearness, which is an ethical force. She noted the progression which begins with people feeling, "We deserve to have a school just as good as the white people's, even if it's a separate school." And by the end of the play they feel: "We deserve to have the *same* school as the white people." That change is an important matter.

4. She said, "The play has roughness, but it is honest. Ossie Davis had a desire to show that there were real people behind a certain occurrence

in history, and you do feel that. There was a sincere dramatic impulsion that should be honored."

This discussion, of which I've quoted only a very little, was important literary criticism. I think Ossie Davis would have felt comprehended, and greatly respected, and I wish he could have been there to hear it.

Aesthetics Is the Answer

What would it mean for people to see persons different from themselves justly? In "Racism Can End," reprinted in this book, Ellen Reiss explains:

Racism won't be effectively done away with unless it is replaced with something that has terrific power. What needs to replace it is not the feeling that the difference of another person is somehow tolerable. What is necessary is the seeing and feeling that the relation of sameness and difference between ourselves and that other person is *beautiful*. People need to feel, with feeling both intimately personal and large, that difference of race is like the difference to be found in music: two notes are different, but they are in behalf of the same melody; they complete each other; each needs the other to be expressed richly, to be fully itself.

Later you will see instances of this answer to racism in the chapter on the teaching method Ruby Dee writes of: the Aesthetic Realism Teaching Method. I know firsthand that through the principles in it, a person comes to see the difference of others not as a threat, but as a means of completing one's own individuality.

Further Documents

After learning about Rev. DeLaine, I became aware of the exhibition "Courage: The South Carolina Story" at the Levine Museum of the New South in Charlotte, North Carolina. It was mounted in 2004 to honor the fiftieth anniversary of *Brown v. Board*. My article on the subject is reprinted here.

Joseph DeLaine, Jr. told me that in 1955, a year after the Supreme Court ruling, the Ku Klux Klan retaliated by burning down his father's church. Joseph DeLaine, Jr.'s account of the brutal "frame up," which forced his father to flee South Carolina for his life, is published here for the first time.

I am moved to conclude this volume with remarks by Ossie Davis from the television show "Speaking Freely" in 2000. During the show, he reflected on the people and events which inspired a lifetime of thought and activism.

Since this book is composed of independent documents, many of which are about the same subject or events, some repetitions are inevitably present. I have chosen to retain these rather than interfere with the integrity of the original works.

I think school children and others will want to perform *The People of Clarendon County*, and teachers will find the script and related documents useful in the classroom. These possibilities pleased Ossie Davis very much.

I hope that through the knowledge in this book people will see history as alive, immediate—and will be encouraged to use both the mistakes and achievements of the past to make the present and future more just!

–Alice Bernstein, April 2007

Dates Relevant to
The People of Clarendon County

1868 – The Fourteenth Amendment to the U.S. Constitution guarantees "equal protection of the laws" to all citizens.

1875 – The U.S. Congress passes the Civil Rights Act to protect the rights of former slaves. The Act states that "all persons within the jurisdiction of the United States shall be entitled to the full and equal enjoyment of the accommodations, advantages, facilities, and privileges of inns, public conveyances on land or water, theaters, and other places of public amusement; subject only to the conditions and limitations established by law, and applicable alike to citizens of every race and color, regardless of any previous condition of servitude."

1883 – The U.S. Supreme Court declares the 1875 Civil Rights Act unconstitutional, ruling that the Fourteenth Amendment applies only to actions by the federal government, not to private individuals or entities. This opens the door for state and local governments to pass laws enforcing racial discrimination—which came to be known as Jim Crow laws.

1896 – In *Plessy v. Ferguson*, an African American, Homer Plessy, loses his challenge to racial discrimination on the railroad. The decision against Plessy provides the legal basis for the doctrine of "separate but equal" in public transportation, accommodations, and schools.

March 16, 1948 – *Levi Pearson v. Clarendon County and School District No. 26* is filed by Levi Pearson, for "equal" school buses for his son and other black children. The case is later dismissed on a technicality.

May 1949–December 1950 – Clarendon County parents, community leader Reverend Joseph DeLaine, and the NAACP begin the process of filing *Briggs v. Elliott*. This petition—named for Harry Briggs, one of twenty parents—against R.W. Elliot, president of the Clarendon County School Board, is for "equal" school buses. The petition is ignored. Then, on December 18, 1950, the parents filed a second petition headed by Harry Briggs, challenging *segregation itself* as unconstitutional.

June 18, 1951 – A three-judge panel at the U.S. District Court in South Carolina rules against the plaintiffs in *Briggs v. Elliott*. The decision upholds school segregation and orders "equalization" of the schools. In his dissenting opinion, Judge J. Waties Waring adamantly opposes segregation as unconstitutional.

October 1951 – Rev. DeLaine's home in Summerton is burned to the ground.

1951–1954 – Because *Briggs v. Elliott* is a constitutional challenge, the NAACP appeals directly to the U.S. Supreme Court. NAACP attorneys, including Harold Boulware and chief counsel Thurgood Marshall, combine *Briggs v. Elliott* with four other school desegregation cases—from the District of Columbia, Virginia, Delaware, and Kansas. These cases are argued collectively before the Supreme Court as *Brown v. Board of Education*.

May 17, 1954 – The Supreme Court rules in *Brown v. Board of Education* that "In the field of public education the doctrine of 'separate but equal' has no place. Separate educational facilities are inherently unequal."

February 1955 – *The People of Clarendon County* by Ossie Davis is performed by Mr. Davis, Ruby Dee, and Sidney Poitier, at Local 1199's union hall in New York City.

October 6, 1955 – St. James Church, where Rev. DeLaine serves as pastor, is "mysteriously" destroyed by fire.

October 10, 1955 – The KKK fires shots into the DeLaine house, provoking a "Shoot Out."

October 11, 1955 – South Carolina authorities issue a warrant for the arrest of Rev. DeLaine, who flees the state.

1956 – Rev. DeLaine charters the DeLaine-Waring AME Church in Buffalo, New York.

August 3, 1974 – Death of Rev. Joseph DeLaine.

November 18, 2003 – A bill is passed by Congress to create Congressional Gold Medals in honor of Rev. DeLaine, Levi Pearson, and Harry and Eliza Briggs.

January 30, 2004 – *"COURAGE: The Carolina Story That Changed America"* at the Levine Museum of the New South opens in honor of *Briggs v. Elliott* and the fiftieth anniversary of *Brown v. Board.*

September 8, 2004 – At a ceremony in Washington, D.C., the Congressional Gold Medals honoring the heroes of Clarendon County are presented to their descendants.

PART ONE

The People of Clarendon County

Ossie Davis

THE PEOPLE OF CLARENDON COUNTY
A SKETCH

NARRATOR: On May 17th, 1954, The Supreme Court of the United States handed down without dissent one of the most significant decisions in its long and eventful history. The Court ruled, that segregation, in public schools, is unconstitutional! Before that, in 17 States, and the District of Columbia, Negroes and whites were required by law to go to separate schools, ride in separate coaches, eat in separate resturants, die in separate hospitals, and get themselves buried as far from each other as possible, in separate graveyards! Yes, Jim Crow has been carried on the southern law books for a long time: since 1896, in fact, when the Supreme Court had ruled that "separate but equal" facilities for white, and for black, did not violate the 14th Amendment. How did it start, this fight which dealt old Jim such a stunning blow? Who were the people that got the whole thing on foot and underway? What were they looking for, what did they seek? Well, the schools in Clarendon County, South Carolina were separate all right, but they certainly weren't equal! And how did the local people feel about it - listen!

DEE: It's wrong, that's what! wrong, wrong, wrong!

POITIER: What's that?

DEE: It's wrong. Did you get enough to eat?

POITIER: Sure Did. Oh man am I tired. (Yawns) Where's Glenn?

DEE: Inside studying. They sent him home from school early today.

POITIER: Early! What's he done this time?

DEE: Nothing - But part of the floor isn't safe. The teacher sent a note. Reverend DeLaine said for you to come on over after supper - and bring your hammer.

Pause   gestured!

POITIER: My Hammer! No! No! I will not. Not again. I work hard all day, each and every day and when I come home I want my rest. I'm not going over to that dangded ol' shack nailing up no boards. Not again!

DEE: This ain't the first time you nailed 'em up.

POITIER: But it's the last time. If they want that shanty patched up let 'em go to the Board of Education. It's their job to keep that school going, not mine.

DEE: Somebody's got to do it. Else the colored won't have no schoolhouse at all. I put your hammer in your overall pocket.

The People of Clarendon County
A Play by Ossie Davis

CAST OF CHARACTERS
Narrator/Rev. Joseph DeLaine
Mary Ragin
William Ragin

NARRATOR: On May 17, 1954, The Supreme Court of the United States handed down without dissent one of the most significant decisions in its long and eventful history. The Court ruled, that segregation, in public schools, is unconstitutional! Before that, in seventeen States, and the District of Columbia, Negroes and whites were required by law to go to separate schools, ride in separate coaches, eat in separate restaurants, die in separate hospitals, and get themselves buried as far from each other as possible, in separate graveyards! Yes, Jim Crow has been carried on the southern law books for a long time: since 1896, in fact, when the Supreme Court had

> *ruled that "separate but equal" facilities for white, and*
> *for black, did not violate the Fourteenth Amendment.*
> *How did it start, this fight which dealt old Jim such a*
> *stunning blow? Who were the people that got the*
> *whole thing on foot and underway? What were they*
> *looking for, what did they seek? Well, the schools in*
> *Clarendon County, South Carolina were separate all*
> *right, but they certainly weren't equal! And how did*
> *the local people feel about it—listen!*

MARY: It's wrong, that's what! Wrong!

WILLIAM: What's that?

MARY: It's wrong. Did you get enough to eat?

WILLIAM: Sure did. Oh man am I tired. (Yawns) Where's Glenn?

MARY: Inside studying. They sent him home from school early today.

WILLIAM: Early! What's he done this time?

MARY: Nothing—But part of the floor isn't safe. The teacher sent a note. Reverend DeLaine said for you to come on over after supper—and bring your hammer.

WILLIAM: My hammer! No! [Pause] Not again. I work hard all day, each and everyday and when I come home I'm tired! I want my rest. I'm not going over to that danged ol' shack, nailing up no boards. Not again!

MARY: This ain't the first time you nailed 'em up.

WILLIAM: But it's the last time. If they want that shanty patched up let 'em go to the Board of Education. It's their job to keep that school going, not mine.

MARY: Somebody's got to do it. Else the colored won't have no school house at all. I put your hammer in your overall pocket.

WILLIAM: You can just take it out again.

MARY: William!

WILLIAM: I tell you I ain't going! I mean that! What you take me for, a mule or something! First it was the chimney, then it was the windows, then it was the roof, next time the doors fell off, and now it's the floor. My advice to them is to burn the whole damn thing down and start from the ground up with a brand new school. I'd help them on that, otherwise, nothing doing.

MARY: William! You listen to me! Glenn's gotta have a decent place to go to school, and so have the other children, all of 'em! And if the white folks won't give it to us—

WILLIAM: Give it to us! Woman, what you mean give? We pay taxes don't we? School ain't nobody's gift, it comes outta people's pockets.

MARY: Well here's Rev. DeLaine now. You tell him about it.

DELAINE: Good evening folks.

MARY &
WILLIAM: Howdy Reverend.

DELAINE: How's Glenn making out?

MARY: Fine as can be. Left up to him, they could tear the school house down altogether and forget the whole thing. All he wants to do is to catch frogs. Won't you set and have a bite?

DELAINE: No thank you, I just finished. Yessuh, I guess Glenn is about like my two little ones when it comes to school. Takes a little time for 'em to appreciate the value of a good education. Well, Brother Ragin, you ready?

WILLIAM: Reverend—I ain't going!

DELAINE: That so, now?

WILLIAM: Reverend DeLaine, I pay my taxes.

DELAINE: And I pay mine.

MARY: And so does everybody else in this county. And that ain't
             all we do, or won't do to see that our children get school-
             ing. Nobody likes that rickety old barn they give us for a
             schoolhouse. But it's the best we got and we'll just have to
             make do 'til the white folks make up their minds.

WILLIAM: I'm sick and tired of waiting on them people to make up
             their minds. They don't have to spend their afternoons bang-
             ing on their school houses.

DELAINE: That's right. I was over in the white section Wednesday.
             They got a brand new building. A gymnasium.

MARY: Yes. And it's all brick. It's pretty.

WILLIAM: While that junk heap we got is thirty years old if it's a day.
             It's a fire trap. Sometimes I think I'd just rather keep Glenn
             at home and teach him myself than send him over there.

DELAINE: It is pretty rickety for a public school.

MARY: And the Board of Education simply refuses to do anything
             about it?

DELAINE: That's right, Mrs. Ragin. Every time we go to 'em about it,
             it's the same old story. They'll fix it for us as soon as they
             can get around to it.

WILLIAM: As soon as they can get around to it. You mean never! We
             pay taxes like everybody else, don't we? Our children got a
             right to a decent schoolhouse.

DELAINE: Ready Brother Ragin?

WILLIAM: Mary! Where'd you put my hammer?

MARY: Where I told you, in your overall pocket.

WILLIAM: I'm getting sick and tired of this run-around they give us.
             You hear me!

MARY: So what you intend to do about it? That's what counts. (Beat)

WILLIAM: I'm gonna *sue* 'em that's what. Every living one of 'em,
             from the Governor on down. Let's go Reverend.

             *NARRATOR: ... And that's how it started; the case
             that made legal history, and rocked the southland to its
             foundation. A little community, fighting to give their
             children a decent education just like everybody else.
             William Ragin, Reverend DeLaine and the men from
             the other families, went on to the schoolhouse and did
             what they had to do, as they had done so many times
             in the past. But this time, they didn't split up and go
             their separate ways home after they finished; this time
             they put their heads together, and went instead to the
             all white Board of Education. They were politely
             received, courteously listened to, and given the same
             old answer.*

WILLIAM: Oh yes! We'll have it fixed up just as soon as we can get
             around to it.

MARY: That's all?

WILLIAM: That's all. "Now you boys got to be a little patient. You'll
             have to wait some." Wait my eye! We tired of waiting! The
             time has come to take steps, and that's just what we done!

MARY: How's that?

9

WILLIAM: We got ourselves a lawyer! And a darn good one, too. NAACP man. Said the only way to get action was to sue!

MARY: Sue! You mean—sue the white folks?

WILLIAM: Sue the Board of Education.

MARY: Is it legal?

WILLIAM: Of course it's legal. You can sue anybody you want to, long as you got a case against them. And we have got a case! Do you know just how much money Negroes in this county pay out in school taxes alone every year?

MARY: Won't it—cost money?

WILLIAM: Of course. But the NAACP lawyer is so interested in the case he's offering his services free. Oh, we told him everything. Laid it right on the line. How the school board gave the white children a brand new gymnasium, while we ain't had a coat of paint since before the war. Ain't but one thing to do, he said. Take 'em to court and *make* 'em give you equal facilities with the whites.

MARY: Make 'em give it to us. We can't make the white folks do nothing.

WILLIAM: Maybe we can't but the law can!

MARY: The law! William the law is one thing for the white man, and another thing for us.

WILLIAM: That's just what the lawyer said is wrong, and we gonna put a stop to it.

MARY: Us, here in Carolina? They won't like it William. They won't like it being sued. Especially by us. You know what they do to people down here who make trouble.

WILLIAM: You call trying to get yourself a decent school making trouble?
Besides this ain't just you and me and Rev. DeLaine.
This is everybody. Every black man, woman and child in
Clarendon County, and if we stick together—

MARY: Will we stick together?

WILLIAM: Of course we will. That's where you come in.

MARY: Me!

WILLIAM: You and Glenn, too—everybody! The lawyer's drawing up
a petition to take into court—that the Negro children in
Clarendon County are being denied equal protection of the
law. Now there's about a thousand parents in this county
with children in school. We want every one of their names
on that petition.

MARY: You think people will sign a thing like that? Our people?

WILLIAM: What have they got to lose?

MARY: You been in the South long as I have, you know good and
well what they got to lose. Their lives!

WILLIAM: Aw Mary!

MARY: You remember those four people killed in Monroe, Georgia
don't you? (pause)

WILLIAM: Yeah! Lined 'em up and shot 'em down like dogs. Never
caught nobody.

MARY: And that soldier, the sheriff put his eyes out... Sometime
when I think about Glenn...and now, this suing the school
board; the white school board.

WILLIAM: But doggone it Mary, I'm thinking 'bout Glenn too. How
much longer you expect me to be able to look Glenn in the
face? How can I look myself in the face if we don't do

11

something?... Well, you want us to go back and tell the lawyer to drop the case?

MARY: (Pause) ... No.

WILLIAM: I know it's a serious thing honey, dead serious. Somebody may get hurt—you, me, maybe even Glenn. If you know of another way, except to fight 'em and keep on fighting them...

MARY: You finish your supper?

WILLIAM: Yeah! Where you going? (Pause—change over)

MARY: If we intend to get a thousand signatures on that petition, we better get a move on...

NARRATOR: And move on they did. One thousand signatures was not easy, but that's what they wanted, and that's what they set out to get. They went to homes, and farms, and churches, lodge meetings, weddings, births, funerals and burials. Wherever two or three colored people happened to get together, that petition was bound to come up from somewhere, and the talk would start. Talk, talk, talk: and pretty soon everybody in Clarendon County was talking....At first, things went very well. But the people had not forgotten about Harry T. Moore in Florida, and those seven innocent boys in Martinsville, Virginia, and Willie McGee. They knew what the South can be like when it takes a mind to. And it made them cautious. And, under constant pressure and threats of blood and violence, even some who had signed changed their minds and took their names off the petition. In fact, by the time they were ready to go into court....

MARY: Twenty-five...twenty-five signatures.

WILLIAM: Twenty-five out of a thousand. Reverend DeLaine... maybe—

DELAINE: Maybe nothing! I'm surprised we got that many! No! I'm
             not surprised—I'm delighted!

MARY: Well—don't keep the lawyer waiting!

WILLIAM: Let's go!

*NARRATOR: On May 16, 1950, the NAACP lawyers
filed suit in the Federal District Court in Charleston,
asking for an injunction "restraining and enjoining the
school board of Clarendon County from making a
distinction on account of race and color in maintaining
public schools for Negro children which are far inferior
to those maintained for the white children." This was
dynamite, and the courthouse was jammed so that the
overflow threatened to block traffic. They came, the
Negroes and the whites, they came and they listened;
hung on every word. For they knew, as the country
itself knew, that what was decided in that court would
affect not only them, but their children's children's
children. And day and night, while it lasted, while they
waited to know—they talked about it, and talked about
it, and talked about it...*

MARY: Rev. DeLaine—Now I've had a fair education, and I can
             hear good enough, and I'll put my understanding up against
             the average person, white or black in Clarendon County. But
             there are certain things the lawyer keeps talking about that
             ain't quite clear to me. He keeps saying the Fourteenth
             Amendment...

DELAINE: Yeah! He says that a lot don't he?

MARY: Yes.

DELAINE: And at first it was a little beyond me, but I had a talk with
             'im, and he give me some papers to read on the subject.
             (Slower) Here...here's one of 'em. You just read that, and

13

	the whole thing'll come clear to you.

MARY: Thank you.

DELAINE: Wait a minute, I want William to hear this too—where is he?

MARY: He took Glenn over to his uncle's this morning. Said he was stopping back by your place.

DELAINE: Well—maybe he did; I ain't been home yet. But read it anyhow, that Fourteenth Amendment to the Constitution of the United States, and get the shock of your life. Read it!

MARY: "Section one. All persons born or naturalized in the United States, and subject to the jurisdiction thereof, are citizens of the United States, and of the state wherein they reside."

DELAINE: Amen! Everybody, and I mean everybody—don't care what: white, red, blue, green, black, brown, or thirteen feet tall— are CITIZENS, CITIZENS! And nobody can't take it away from 'em. Read on.

MARY: "No State shall make, or enforce, any law which shall abridge the privileges and immunities of citizens of the United States."

DELAINE: Daughter—that means what it says! South Carolina, North Carolina, or no other Carolina can make a law to cut you off from your rights and privileges. Even if you are a Negro. Read on.

MARY: "Nor shall any state deprive any person of life, liberty, or property without due process of law—"

DELAINE: Due process of law. That means fair trial, out in the open, with witnesses and cross examination. Now what about them two boys they just executed last year for rape? Their mother swears they never left the house that night, and even the woman herself later said she made a mistake. The state took

14

their lives for one reason—they were black.

MARY: It was murder! Cold-blooded murder!

DELAINE: Ah, but there's a new wind blowing through this country and
               things are gonna be a lot different from here on, you just
               bet your life on it. Read some more!

MARY: "No state shall deny to any person within its jurisdiction the
               equal protection of the law."

DELAINE: The equal protection of the law. Amen, amen, amen. That
               means that in the eyes of the law, every man stands equal.
               Like the lawyer said. Listen. This is what a famous Supreme
               Court judge once said. I committed it to memory: "Our
               Constitution is color blind, and neither knows nor tolerates
               classes among citizens. In respect of Civil Rights, all citizens
               are equal before the law. The law regards man as man, and
               takes no account of his surrounding, or of his color." In other
               words, if we all pay taxes together we should all go to
               school together.

MARY: That's what it says.

DELAINE: And no state, no state can make or enforce any law that
               says different.

MARY: That's right, Reverend.

DELAINE: Now look at this. This is Article Eleven of the South
               Carolina State Constitution. Read it!

MARY: "Separate schools shall be provided for children of the white
               and colored races, and no child of either race shall ever be
               permitted to attend a school provided for children of the
               other."

DELAINE: You see it? You get it? South Carolina got two laws: one
               for whites, and another for black. —But the Fourteenth

15

Amendment to the Federal Constitution says there can't be but one law, the same law—for white and for black. And no state can deny anybody the equal protection of that one law!

MARY: But, Rev. DeLaine. How long has this amendment been in the Constitution?

DELAINE: July 28, 1868.

MARY: You mean to tell me, segregation and discrimination have been illegal all these years?

DELAINE: That's what the lawyer told them three judges in court.

MARY: Eighty some odd years of Jim Crow, and all the time it was against the Constitution of the United States!

DELAINE: Yes, but that was in the past. Things gonna be different now. Like the lawyer said—you can't have segregation and the Constitution too. One of 'em has got to go.

MARY: You think they'll listen to a colored lawyer in the South! They dodged the Constitution all these years, I don't see 'em changing now.

DELAINE: We'll make 'em change! If not in this court, then in a higher one. If not in the courts, then in Congress.

MARY: And if not in Congress?

DELAINE: We'll take it to the place where Congress comes from—the people.

WILLIAM: (Breaking in) Rev. DeLaine! Rev. DeLaine!

DELAINE: William what is—

WILLIAM: Run Reverend! Run! They done set your house on fire!

DELAINE: Merciful Redeemer!

MARY: William, William! Call the fire department.

WILLIAM: We called them already. Come on, let's go! Let's go!

> *NARRATOR: They all ran out of the house and down the road towards Rev. DeLaine's house, black silhouettes against a background of angry flames. Luckily, the blaze had been discovered early, and in a short while the fire trucks, sirens screaming and bells clanging, roared to a halt in front of the burning building. The firemen dismounted and leapt into action. But the chief, who had found out by this time whose house it was, ordered the hose back onto the trucks.*

WILLIAM: Hey!... Hey!

MARY: William, William! What are they doing?

WILLIAM: They're leaving!

MARY: But the house! What about the house!

DELAINE: My house…it's my house. Save my house!

WILLIAM: Hey! Fire Department. Come back here! Come back here!

> *NARRATOR: But the chief, and all his men, and his trucks, and his hose and his hooks and ladders, pumps and whatnot, turned around and roared away to the city without even looking back.*

WILLIAM: Buckets everybody! Everybody get buckets, and we'll make a chain from here to the well.

MARY: William, the wind is shifting.

WILLIAM: Faster, everybody, faster! Faster! Faster!

MARY: The wall! Look out! (Screams)

*NARRATOR: But all to no avail…The house burned
completely to the ground and everything in it was
utterly destroyed…. To this day, nobody knows how it
started, or who it was that started it….But later…they
found out why the fire chief brought his equipment all
the way out to Rev. DeLaine's house, and wouldn't
use it.*

WILLIAM: You saw the chief? What did he say?

DELAINE: My house is beyond the city limits.

WILLIAM: What? Of course your house is beyond the city limits.

DELAINE: And, he's not required to fight any fires beyond the city line.

WILLIAM: Well I'll be…They do it all the time. Last year, when the
            Peters' barn caught on fire…

MARY: Peters is white!

WILLIAM: By God, Rev. DeLaine, that's wrong. That department
            belongs to the taxpayers and it's supposed to serve the
            interest of the taxpayers!

MARY: You mean, equal protection of the law.
            How do you suppose it started?

WILLIAM: It was set, that's what. They done it to scare us off.

MARY: Suppose you'da been caught inside, upstairs, or if the
            children hadn't been to their grandma's.

DELAINE: I thought about that. Seems like they'll stop at nothing. I
            went to the sheriff, to ask him to come out and investigate.

WILLIAM: What he say?

DELAINE: Soon as he can get around to it.

WILLIAM: Soon as he can get around to it. Don't he think we got no rights at all!

DELAINE: Don't look like it.

WILLIAM: By God and by Jesus, ain't but one thing to do. Sue 'em. Sue the whole she bang from the governor on down. And that fire chief. It's criminal, that's what it is. Ain't but one way to teach them respect for the law. Sue 'em!

MARY: That's all you can talk about. Suing. Ain't we got trouble enough already from suing the white folks. You want 'em to burn us all up! I wish to God we'd never started this whole thing in the first place. We can't win! What's the use of fooling ourselves?

DELAINE: Didn't you hear about the verdict?

WILLIAM: Yeah—didn't you hear?

MARY: First it was your place, then, who knows. Maybe we're next!

WILLIAM: Mary!

MARY: All these old frame houses…go up so fast, wouldn't know what hit you.

WILLIAM: Mary, cut it out!

MARY: Who's to stop 'em? They own the law, the courts, the governors, the presidents, the sheriffs, the fire department. What's to stop them from burning down every house on the place if they want to, they could go with a mob, like in Columbus, Tennessee, or maybe wait out there 'til it's dark and slip in and blow our brains out or cut our throats while we sleep…

WILLIAM: Stop it Mary….Stop it! You getting yourself all riled up.

19

DELAINE: No need upsetting yourself like that…

MARY: (Crying) I just want my baby to go to school, that's all, just to go to school.

WILLIAM: He is going to school.

DELAINE: And a better one. Didn't you hear about the court's decision? They got to give us everything equal to the white schools, everything!

MARY: They do?

WILLIAM: The state's already floating a $75 million dollar bond issue, just to bring Negro schools up to date.

MARY: ….William.

WILLIAM: We won, honey, we won!

DELAINE: We didn't.

WILLIAM: We didn't!

DELAINE: I don't care if they gave us a school out of fourteen carat gold, as long as it's segregated, it's unequal, it's inferior, it violates my rights under the Fourteenth Amendment and I won't have it. The big fight is still ahead of us.

MARY: Big fight? But we been fighting…I'm tired, just tired!

DELAINE: This ain't the kind of battle we can afford to get tired in.

MARY: Then I'm not tired, I'm scared!

DELAINE: That's no excuse, everybody's scared!

MARY: But Reverend DeLaine, you just said they got to give us a better school.

WILLIAM: Yeah, and if it's as good as theirs, well, that's what we started out to get, ain't it?

DELAINE: How can it be as good long as it's segregated! The lawyer is already drawing up the papers to appeal to the Supreme Court.

WILLIAM: The Supreme Court! In Washington?

DELAINE: That's right. But he can't do a thing without our consent because it's our case.

WILLIAM: The Supreme Court—I mean, let's look at this. I didn't expect to get as much as we did get!

MARY: Yes. No need biting off more than we can chew Rev. I think we done enough for one time. Better leave well enough alone.

DELAINE: It ain't well enough, and it won't be 'til white boys and girls and black boys and girls sit side by side in the same room. Anything else is not equality and against the Constitution.

MARY: No law in all this world will ever make 'em do that.

DELAINE: They'll have to do it or get left far behind the times. And besides, we aren't the only ones with a case like this. There's one in Topeka, Kansas; Prince Edward County, Virginia; Delaware; and the District of Columbia. Are we gonna be the only slackers in the lot?

WILLIAM: But Reverend, them people are up north practically, and we're in South Carolina.

MARY: That's right. And don't forget what they done to your house.

DELAINE: Ain't no house in the world worth my rights under the Constitution. They'll have to burn down more than that to scare me off. I tell you, we got them on the run, condemned

21

before the entire civilized world, we can't stop now. Things have changed. Out of the three judges, one voted against segregation!

MARY: Voted against it. A white man?

DELAINE: A white man.

WILLIAM: A Carolina white man?

DELAINE: From one of the oldest families in the state. Listen: "The Supreme Court has clearly recognized, in the case of *Sweat versus Painter*, that education does not alone consist of fine buildings, classroom furniture, and appliances, but that included in education must be all the intangibles that come into play in preparing one for meeting life. Racial prejudice is something that is acquired in early childhood. If segregation is wrong, then the place to stop it is not in the graduate college, but in the first grade….Further, if Negroes are entitled to any rights as American citizens, they are entitled to have these rights, not in the future, but now!"

WILLIAM: What was his name?

DELAINE: J. Waties Waring.

MARY: I never thought I'd live to see this day.

DELAINE: This is my battle and nobody's gonna beat me fighting for my own rights. I'm seeing this thing to the end. Are you with me?

WILLIAM: I can't imagine nothing that would make me any prouder.

MARY: And me too, Rev. DeLaine.

DELAINE: Good! We'll take this thing to the Supreme Court, and we'll

22

keep it there 'til Carolina and all the other Southern states come back into the human race. And believe me—this is just the first step!

End

PART TWO

Photographs and Historical Documents,
and Essays on the Education That Can End Racism

Photograph Album

(l-r) Mattie DeLaine and Helen Richburg with their students in front of Spring Hill School, circa 1938-39. This structure was built as a lodge hall by members of the congregation of the adjacent church–Spring Hill A.M.E. It is typical of the makeshift quarters that black students were forced to occupy when no South Carolina tax money was allocated to building African American school buildings.

(Photo courtesy of the DeLaine family.)

Liberty Hill School, one of the black schools in the *Briggs v. Elliott* lawsuit.
Rev. DeLaine stands at the right.
(South Carolina State Archives, Courtesy of the Levine Museum of the New South.)

Summerton Graded, one of the white schools involved in the *Briggs v. Elliott* lawsuit.
(South Carolina State Archives. Courtesy of the Levine Museum of the New South.)

NAACP poster, 1946

Clarendon County Parents and Children

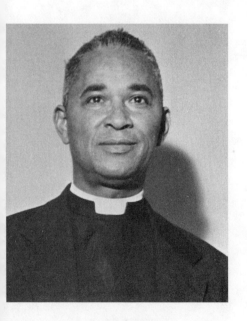

Rev. DeLaine

Rev. and Mrs. Mattie DeLaine

Levi Pearson   *Bennie Parson*

Briggs v. Elliott parents and children. Two photos:
(*Courtesy of Cecil J. Williams. Out-of-the-Box in Dixie.*)

Hazel Ragin, Joseph DeLaine, Edward Ragin

Eliza and Harry Briggs with Rev. DeLaine in 1962,
after they were forced to flee South Carolina.
(Courtesy of Cecil J. Williams.
Out-of-the-Box in Dixie.)

Reverdy Wells

Susan Lawson

Rebecca Richburg

R. Georgia

Lee Richardson

Bo Stukes

Lucresia Richardson

Henry Scott

Annie Gibson

Rev. DeLaine at the pulpit.
(Photo is by E.C. Jones, Jr. and is from the
DeLaine Family collection. Courtesy of the
Levine Museum of the New South)

Judge J. Waties Waring.
(Photograph by Fabian Bachrach. Courtesy of
Joseph DeLaine, Jr. and South Caroliniana
Library, University of South Carolina,)

Key ministers involved in *Briggs v. Elliott* movement. (l-r) Reverends Edward Frazier, James W. Seals, Joseph
DeLaine, and Edward Richburg.
(Courtesy of J.A. DeLaine, Jr.)

Rev. J.A. DeLaine and his family in 1951, standing beside the ruins of their home.
Joseph A. DeLaine Papers.
(Courtesy of South Caroliniana Library. University of South Carolina, Columbia.)

*Thurgood Marshall in 1951, then age
43, NAACP attorney, later a U.S.
Supreme Court Justice. Here he arrives
on the Silver Meteor train in Charleston
to prepare for court.
(Courtesy of Cecil J. Williams.
Out-of-the-Box in Dixie.)*

*AME Bishops on steps of the Supreme Court prior to the
May 17, 1954, decision announcement.
(Courtesy of J.A. DeLaine, Jr.)*

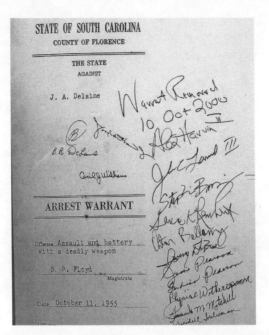

1955 arrest warrant issued by the State of South Carolina for Rev. J.A. DeLaine. Handwritten note states the warrant was removed October 10, 2000.
(Courtesy of Cecil J. Williams. Out-of-the-Box in Dixie.)

1956 Madison Square Garden Freedom Rally. (l-r) Roger Wilkins, Gus Courts (Mississippi), Rev. DeLaine, Eleanor Roosevelt, Autherine Lucy (Alabama), and actress Tallulah Bankhead.
(Courtesy of Cecil J. Williams. Out-of-the-Box in Dixie.)

Historic Marker. Liberty Hill Church at the church one mile north of St. Paul, on County Road 373, South Carolina. In 1867, five years after the Emancipation Proclamation, Thomas and Margaret Briggs gave four acres of land to the African Methodist Episcopal Church. The present building, completed in 1905, has been brick veneered. Meetings held here in the 1940s and 1950s led to local court cases, which helped bring about the U.S. Supreme Court's 1954 ruling desegregating public schools.

Photo of "Courage" exhibitition installation showing original signers of *Briggs v. Elliott* petition. *(Courtesy of John Hilarides, the Levine Museum of the New South.)*

Reverse side reads: Pioneers in Desegregation Nineteen members of this congregation were plaintiffs in the case of *Harry Briggs, Jr. v. R.W. Elliott*, heard in U.S. District Court, Charleston, in 1952. Although this court refused to abolish racial segregation in S.C. schools, this case, with others, led to the U.S. Supreme Court's 1954 landmark decision desegregating public schools. Erected by the Congregation, 1985.

Viola Pearson holds the Congressional Medal

2004 Congressional Medal ceremonies (l-r standing) then-House Minority Leader Nancy Pelosi, Nathaniel Briggs, Senator Ernst "Fritz" Hollings, Congressman James Clyburn, Joseph DeLaine, Jr. (seated) Viola Pearson and her son Ferdinand Pearson.
(Photos courtesy of Cecil J. Williams and Congressman James E. Clyburn)

Photographs of Ossie Davis, Ruby Dee, Sidney Poitier, and Moe Foner

Moe Foner, Ruby Dee, Ossie Davis.
(Courtesy of Dee and Davis Archive.)

Ruby Dee and Sidney Poitier, in A Raisin in the Sun, 1959.
(Courtesy of Philip Rose.)

Local 1199 Award to Ossie Davis in 1964. (l-r) Ricardo Montalban,
Ossie Davis, Moe Foner, Leon J. Davis.
(Courtesy of Dee and Davis Archives.)

Ossie Davis (front, in Fedora) and Leon J. Davis (center with glasses), founder of 1199, at 1965 strike,
Lawrence Hospital, Bronxville, NY.
(Courtesy of 1199 News.)

Ossie Davis and Moe Foner in 1979.
(Courtesy of Dee and Davis Archives.)

Alice Neel, Ossie Davis, Moe Foner, and E.L. Doctorow, looking at William King's
sculpture, "A. Lincoln" at Bread & Roses "Images of Labor" exhibition in 1981.
(Courtesy of Dee and Davis Archives.)

Stills from the February 2004 production of *The Seat of Justice by* Julian Wiles of Charleston Stage (about *Briggs v. Elliott)*

Thurgood Marshall and John Davis meet with Federal Judge Waties Waring in a pretrial hearing for Briggs v. Elliott.
(Courtesy of Charleston Stage.)

Psychologist Dr. Kenneth Clark testifies.
(Courtesy of Charleston Stage.)

Thurgood Marshall and John Davis meet with Federal Judge Waties Waring
in a pretrial hearing for *Briggs v. Elliott.*
(*Courtesy of Charleston Stage.*)

The parents's petition is signed.
(*Courtesy of Charleston Stage.*)

2 Brown v. Board of Education: What Interferes with Justice?
ALICE BERNSTEIN

As America commemorates the fiftieth anniversary of the Supreme Court decision *Brown v. the Board of Education*, the question of what interferes with justice is as alive as ever. The 1954 decision was momentous in stating that "separate educational facilities are inherently unequal" and unconstitutional. The Court later added that these inequities should be rectified "with all deliberate speed."

While strides have been made towards racial integration and civil rights, public education today is still in crisis. Most black students—North and South—attend inferior schools in which they are a majority. "If you really believe in *Brown*, you can't celebrate it right now," states Gary Orfield, director of the Harvard Project on School Desegregation *(New York Times)*. "But the potential is there."

We have to ask ourselves: Why, in these fifty years, has there not been more progress towards equality and justice? What in people is opposed to it?

I am convinced the answers lie in Aesthetic Realism. Eli Siegel explained the constant question in a person's life: whether to know and respect the world and other people or contemptuously look down on them in order to build ourselves up. He saw that contempt, "the addition to self through the lessening of something else," is the cause of every injustice. Contempt has thousands of forms, as common as a sneer, or a man's thinking he knows more than all his wife's relatives, or a feeling of indifference to another's distress. Yet the same ordinary contempt in people has led to cross burnings, lynchings, economic injustice, and war.

At the present time we, as individuals, and as a nation, have to ask what represents us. Will it be the contemptuous desire to feel other lives are inferior, or the desire for justice? "However idealistic it may sound," Mr. Siegel wrote, "a person not caring enough for justice cannot be definitely happy. Justice is the great opponent of contempt; justice, loved and studied, can in time have a victory over contempt."

Brown v. Board was an important step. We should use it now to study justice and ask how much we care for it.

South Carolina: *Briggs v. Board of Education*

The African American community in South Carolina can be immensely proud that the *Brown* case began in 1947 in Clarendon County. Reverend Joseph Armstrong DeLaine, a local school teacher and country preacher, joined by other African American parents, filed complaints, petitions, and the first lawsuit in behalf of equal education for their children. Photographs of black and white schools at the time show vividly that separate was definitely not equal.

This history comes alive at the Levine Museum of the New South exhibition designed by Darcie Fohrman with historian Tom Hanchett, "Courage: The South Carolina Story That Changed America." Visitors can have a seat in a "Black Classroom" —two chairs placed apart with a plank of wood between. There, students used worn out books discarded by white schools and marked "For Colored Use Only." On display are firsthand accounts and photographs of people who attended these schools. Henry Lawson, for instance, tells of his school, without plumbing or heating: "In winter we had to go into the woods to get something to burn."

In the international journal, *The Right of Aesthetic Realism to Be Known*, (issue #635) Ellen Reiss presents these questions a person should ask himself or herself:

> Are the feelings of other people as real to you as your own? Are you interested in what people of [another race] are really hoping for, or would you like an answer that makes you comfortable and superior? If a person's color is different from yours, do you feel your difference is more or less than your sameness?

These questions are a means of understanding why many white people, with tender feelings for their own children, were so cruelly unjust to others.

Heroism, Good Will, and the Answer to Racism

In 1948, Rev. Joseph DeLaine led a group of parents in Summerton, South Carolina in filing a lawsuit—*Levi Pearson v. Clarendon County and School District No. 26*—for equal school buses for their children. This case, the first of its kind, was thrown out on a technicality. Undaunted, the parents continued their petitions and suits. After years of case dismissals and stonewalling by the courts, in 1951 the Clarendon County African American community, with the help of the NAACP Legal Defense Fund, filed *Briggs v. Elliott* not just for a bus, but for equal schools. This pioneering case was later joined by other lawsuits from Delaware, District of Columbia, Virginia, and Kansas, and organized by Thurgood Marshall, of the NAACP Legal Defense Fund, into *Brown v. Board of Education.*

When called upon by his neighbors to be their spokesman in the first lawsuit, Rev. DeLaine is reported to have said, "The only way that I will accept this is if you are willing to go all the way to the Supreme Court. And it ain't going to be easy. There may even be killing."

He was right. Reprisals on Rev. DeLaine and the other brave parents were fast and extreme—whites called it "The Squeeze." People who were already poor and working as servants, farmers and laborers lost their jobs and their land. Homes were burned, and the one white federal judge who ruled in their favor—Justice J. Waties Waring—was given such a hard time, including by his own family, that he was forced to leave the South.

The best thing in every person, Aesthetic Realism explains, is the feeling that we take care of ourselves by giving justice to others. This is good will, "the desire to have something else stronger and more beautiful, for this desire makes oneself stronger and more beautiful," and far from being soft and weak, it is the toughest thing in this world! It is the only alternative to contempt. I believe the heroism of Rev. DeLaine and many others arose from good will that was courageous and mighty.

When he wouldn't back down, in 1955, Rev. DeLaine was given an ultimatum by the Ku Klux Klan to leave town in ten days or die. He fled South Carolina. (See Chapter 4, Concerning the "Shoot Out.")

He went to Buffalo, New York, where he and his wife, Mattie, taught school. I was tremendously moved to learn that in 1956 Rev. DeLaine chartered the DeLaine-Waring AME Church—named in honor of Judge Waring. Though Rev. DeLaine wished to return to the land and people he loved, and despite the pleas of many people, the state refused to withdraw the warrant for his arrest and he was prohibited from setting foot in South Carolina. He died in Charlotte, North Carolina, in 1974.

Within the Feelings of Others

The Levine Museum's "Courage" exhibition does something urgently needed: It encourages visitors to get within the feelings of other people and, in doing so, become deeper and kinder. On display is a large copy of the original *Briggs v. Elliott* petition with pictures of the people who signed it. The museum's communications manager, Ashley Thurmond, told me: "As we began collecting pictures from around 1949 when they signed the [first] petition, our exhibit and research team discovered many signatures came from students, young people. We have a copy of the petition beside the enlarged original, with lines and a pen for museum visitors to sign their names. The caption states, 'The signers of the petition risked everything—their homes, their jobs, their safety. Would you sign your name?'"

Julie, a thirteen-year-old student visiting this exhibit, told *The Charlotte Observer:* "I thought it was cool to see that people who signed the petition were kids our age. And I thought, if that same situation happened now, would I have enough courage to stand up for what I was thinking?" It is a good question for everyone. "Man will not be fully human," wrote Eli Siegel, "until he is interested in justice with great intensity and with the comprehensiveness which does not wish to miss any of its forms."

[This article appeared in the South Carolina Black News *and many other newspapers in 2004, and refers to an exhibition at the Levine Museum of the New South (Charlotte, North Carolina).]*

3 Dissenting Opinion, *Briggs v. Elliott*
JUDGE J. WATIES WARING

Judge J. Waties Waring (1880-1968) was a native of Charleston, South Carolina and came from a family who traced its history there for two hundred years. In his early career as a judge he was a segregationist like the other white judges in South Carolina. But he came to see things differently and changed— after that, there was no turning back. Of the three-judge panel which decided against the parents in the 1951 Briggs v. Elliott *case, his was the dissenting opinion. As a civil rights activist, he put his life on the line. His own family would have nothing to do with him. Eventually he was run out of town, and he and his second wife, Elizabeth, settled in New York City. When the Supreme Court's* Brown v. Board *decision came down in 1954, the Warings threw a big party in their home on Fifth Avenue.*

Rev. DeLaine corresponded with the judge from his new home in Buffalo, New York. In one letter dated July 6, 1956, Judge Waring wrote: "I have your letter and am glad that you have been assigned to organize an A.M.E. Church in Buffalo. It is a great relief to your friends to know that you have found a place where you can be safe from the racial persecution of the deep South. I note that you...suggest naming your new Church 'DeLaine-Waring.' I not only approve but am deeply moved at this honor, which however undeserved, I accept with thanks. And I wish you the greatest of success in your new endeavor."

What follows are excerpts from Judge Waring's dissenting opinion in Briggs v. Elliott. In it he considers the history of segregation from ancient times to the present to explain his position against the Board of Education (R.W. Elliott, et al.) and in favor of the parents and children of Clarendon County.

As Judge Waring's dissenting opinion builds, the writing in it becomes powerful: It puts together passionate feeling and clear logic. He is described in Tinsley E. Yarbrough's biography as "the first jurist in modern times to declare that 'segregation is per se inequality.'"

From Dissenting Opinion, *Briggs v. Elliott*
June 1951
by Judge J. Waties Waring

In the District Court of the United States
Fourth Eastern District of South Carolina
Charleston Division

Harry Briggs, Jr., et al, Plaintiffs
v.
R.W. Elliott, Chairman, et al, Defendants

This case has been brought for the express and declared purpose of determining the right of the State of South Carolina, in its public schools, to practice segregation according to race.

The Plaintiffs are all residents of Clarendon County, South Carolina, which is situated within the Eastern District of South Carolina and within the jurisdiction of this court. The Plaintiffs consist of minors and adults, there being forty-six minors who are qualified to attend and are attending the public schools in School District Twenty-two of Clarendon County; and twenty adults who are taxpayers and are either guardians or parents of the minor Plaintiffs. The Defendants are members of the Board of Trustees of School District Twenty-two and other officials of the educational system of Clarendon County including the superintendent of education. They are the parties in charge of the various schools which are situated within the aforesaid school district and which are affected by the matters set forth in this cause.

The Plaintiffs allege that they are discriminated against by the Defendants under cover of the Constitution and laws of the State of South Carolina whereby they are denied equal educational facilities and opportunities and that this denial is based upon difference in race. And they show that the school system of this particular school district and county (following the general pattern that it is admitted obtains in the State of South Carolina) sets up two classes of schools; one for people said to belong to the white race and the other for people of other races but primarily for those said to belong to the Negro race or of mixed races and either wholly, partially, or faintly alleged to be of African or Negro descent. These Plaintiffs bring this action for the enforcement of the rights to which they claim they are entitled....

It appears that the Plaintiffs filed a petition with the Defendants requesting that the Defendants cease discrimination against the Negro children of public school age; and the situation complained of not having been remedied or changed, the Plaintiffs now ask this court to require the Defendants to grant them their rights guaranteed under the Fourteenth Amendment of the Constitution of the United States and they appeal to the equitable power of this court for declaratory and injunctive relief alleging that they are suffering irreparable injuries and that they have no plain, adequate or complete remedy to redress the wrongs and illegal acts complained of other than this suit. And they further point out that large numbers of people and persons are and will be affected by the decision of this court in adjudicating and clarifying the rights of Negroes to obtain education in the public school system of the State of South Carolina without discrimination and denial of equal facilities on account of their race.

The Defendants appear and by way of answer deny the allegations of the Complaint as to discrimination and inequality and allege that not only are they acting within the laws of the State in enforcing segregation but that all facilities afforded the pupils of different races are adequate and equal and that there is no inequality or discrimination practiced against these Plaintiffs or any others by reason of race or color. And they allege that the facilities and opportunities furnished to the colored children are substantially the same as those provided for the white children. And they further base their defense upon the statement that the Constitutional and statutory provisions under attack in this case, that is to say, the provisions requiring separate schools because of race, are a reasonable exercise of the State's police power and that all of the same are valid under the powers possessed by the State of South Carolina and the Constitution of the United States and they deny that the same can be held to be unconstitutional by this Court....

The case came on for a trial upon the issues as presented in the Complaint and Answer. But upon the call of the case, Defendants' counsel announced that they wished to make a statement on behalf of the Defendants making certain admissions and praying that the Court make a finding as to inequalities in respect to buildings, equipment, facilities, curricula and other aspects of the schools provided for children in School District Twenty-two in Clarendon County and giving the public authorities time to formulate plans for ending such inequalities. In this statement Defendants claim that they never had intended to discriminate against any of the pupils and although they had filed an answer to the Complaint, some five months ago, denying inequalities, they now admit that they had found some; but rely upon the fact that subsequent to the institution of this suit, James F. Byrnes, the Governor of South Carolina, had stated in his inaugural address that the State must take steps to provide money for improving educational facilities and that thereafter, the Legislature had adopted certain legislation. They stated that they hoped that in time they would obtain money as a result of the foregoing and improve the school situation.

This statement was allowed to be filed and considered as an amendment to the answer.

By this maneuver, the Defendants have endeavored to induce this Court to avoid the primary purpose of the suit. And if the Court should follow this suggestion and fail to meet the issues raised by merely considering this case in the light of another "separate but equal" case, the entire purpose and reason for the institution of the case and the convening of a three-judge court would be voided. The sixty-six Plaintiffs in this case have brought this suit at what must have cost much in effort and financial expenditures. They are here represented by six attorneys, all, save one, practicing lawyers from without the State of South Carolina and coming here from a considerable distance. The Plaintiffs have brought a large number of witnesses exclusive of themselves. As a matter of fact, they called and examined eleven witnesses. They said that they had a number more coming who did not arrive in time owing to the shortening of the proceedings and they also stated that they had on hand and had contemplated calling a large number of other witnesses but this became unnecessary by reason of the foregoing admissions by Defendants. It certainly appears that large expenses must have been caused by the institution of this case and great efforts expended in gathering data, making a study of the issues involved, interviewing and bringing numerous witnesses, some of whom are foremost scientists in America. And in addition to all of this, these sixty-six Plaintiffs have not merely expended their time and money in order to test this important Constitutional question, but they have shown unexampled courage in bringing and presenting this case at their own expense in the face of the long established and age-old pattern of the way of life which the State of South Carolina has adopted and practiced and lived in since and as a result of the institution of human slavery.

If a case of this magnitude can be turned aside and a court refuse to hear these basic issues by the mere device of an admission that some buildings, blackboards, lighting fixtures and toilet facilities are unequal but that they may be remedied by the spending of a few dollars, then, indeed people in the plight in which these Plaintiffs are, have no adequate remedy or forum in which to air their wrongs. If this method of judicial evasion be adopted, these very infant Plaintiffs now pupils in Clarendon County will probably be bringing suits for their children and grandchildren decades or rather generations hence in an effort to get for their descendants what are today denied to them. If they are entitled to any rights as American citizens, they are entitled to have these rights now and not in the future. And no excuse can be made to deny them these rights which are theirs under the Constitution and laws of America by the use of the false doctrine and patter called "separate but equal" and it is the duty of the Court to meet these issues simply and factually and without fear, sophistry and evasion. If this be the measure of justice to be meted out to them, then, indeed, hundreds, nay thousands, of cases will have to be brought and in each case thousands of dollars will have to be spent for the employment of legal talent and scientific testimony and then the cases will be turned aside, postponed or eliminated by devices such as this.

We should be unwilling to straddle or avoid this issue and if the suggestion made by these Defendants is to be adopted as the type of justice to be meted out by this Court, then I want no part of it.

And so we must and do face, without evasion or equivocation, the question as to whether segregation in education in our schools is legal or whether it cannot exist under our American system as particularly enunciated in the Fourteenth Amendment to the Constitution of the United States.

Before the American Civil War, the institution of human slavery had been adopted and was approved in this country. Slavery was nothing new in the world. From the dawn of history we see aggressors enslaving weak and less fortunate neighbors. Back through the days of early civilizations man practiced slavery. We read of it in Biblical days; we read of it in the Greek City States and in the great Roman Empire. Throughout medieval Europe, forms of slavery existed and it was widely practiced in Asia Minor and the Eastern countries and perhaps reached its worst form in Nazi Germany. Class and caste have, unfortunately, existed through the ages. But, in time, mankind, through evolution and progress, through ethical and religious concepts, through the study of the teachings of the great philosophers and the great religious teachers, including especially the founder of Christianity, mankind began to revolt against the enslavement of body, mind and soul of one human being by another. And so there came about a great awakening. The British, who had indulged in the slave trade, awakened to the fact that it was immoral and against the right thinking ideology of the Christian world. And in this country, also, came about a moral awakening. Unfortunately, this had not been sufficiently advanced at the time of the adoption of the American Constitution for the institution of slavery to be prohibited. But there was a struggle and the better thinking leaders in our Constitutional Convention endeavored to prohibit slavery but unfortunately compromised the issue on the insistent demands of those who were engaged in the slave trade and purchase and use of slaves. And so as time went on, slavery was perpetuated and eventually became a part of the life and culture of certain of the States of this Union although the rest of the world looked on with shame and abhorrence.

As was so well said, this country could not continue to exist one-half slave and one-half free and long years of war were entered into before the nation was willing to eradicate this system which was, itself, a denial of the grave and fine statements of the Declaration of Independence and denial of freedom as envisioned and advocated by our Founders.

The United States then adopted the Thirteenth, Fourteenth and Fifteenth Amendments and it cannot be denied that the basic reason for all of these Amendments to the Constitution was to wipe out completely the institution of slavery and to declare that all citizens in this country should be considered as free, equal and entitled to all of the provisions of citizenship.

The Fourteenth Amendment to the Constitution of the United States is as follows:

Section 1. All persons born or naturalized in the United States, and subject to the jurisdiction thereof, are citizens of the United States and of the State wherein they reside. No State shall make or enforce any law which shall abridge the privileges or immunities of citizens of the United States; nor shall any State deprive any person of life, liberty, or property, without due process of law; nor deny to any person within its jurisdiction the equal protection of the laws.

It seems to me that it is unnecessary to pore through voluminous arguments and opinions to ascertain what the foregoing means. And while it is true that we have had hundreds, perhaps thousands, of legal opinions outlining and defining the various effects and overtones on our laws and life brought about by the adoption of this Amendment, one of ordinary ability and understanding of the English language will have no trouble in knowing that when this Amendment was adopted, it was intended to do away with discrimination between our citizens.

The Amendment refers to *all* persons. There is nothing in there that attempts to separate, segregate or discriminate against any persons because of their being of European, Asian or African ancestry. And the plain intendment is that all of these persons are citizens. And then it is provided that no State shall make or enforce any law which shall abridge the privileges of citizens nor shall any state deny "to any person within its jurisdiction the equal protection of the laws."

The Amendment was first proposed in 1866 just about a year after the end of the American Civil War and the Surrender of the Confederate States government. Within two years, the Amendment was adopted and became part of the Constitution of the United States. It cannot be gainsaid that the Amendment was proposed and adopted wholly and entirely as a result of the great conflict between freedom and slavery. This will be amply substantiated by an examination and appreciation of the proposal and discussion and Congressional debates (*See* Flack on Adoption of the Fourteenth Amendment) and so it is undeniably true that the three great Amendments were adopted to eliminate not only slavery, itself, but all idea of discrimination and difference between American citizens.

Let us now come to consider whether the Constitution and Laws of the State of South Carolina which we have heretofore quoted are in conflict with the true meaning and intendment of this Fourteenth Amendment. The whole discussion of race and ancestry has been intermingled with sophistry and prejudice. What possible definition can be found for the so-called white race, Negro race or other races? Who is to decide and what is the test? For years, there was much talk of blood and taint of blood. Science tells us that there are but four kinds of blood: A, B, AB and O and these are found in Europeans, Asiatics, Africans, Americans and others.

And so we need not further consider the irresponsible and baseless references to preservation of "Caucasian blood." So then, what test are we going to use in opening our school doors and labeling them "white" and "Negro"? The law of South Carolina considers a person of one-eighth African ancestry to be a Negro. Why this proportion? Is it based upon any reason: anthropological, historical or ethical? And how are the trustees to know who are "whites" and who are "Negroes"? If it is dangerous and evil for a white

57

child to be associated with another child, one of whose great-grandparents was of African descent, is it not equally dangerous for one with a one-sixteenth percentage? And if the State has decided that there is danger in contact between the whites and Negroes, isn't it requisite and proper that the State furnish a series of schools one for each of these percentages? If the idea is perfect racial equality in educational systems, why should children of pure African descent be brought in contact with children of one-half, one-fourth, or one-eighth such ancestry? To ask these questions is sufficient answer to them. The whole thing is unreasonable, unscientific and based upon unadulterated prejudice. We see the results of all of this warped thinking in the poor under-privileged and frightened attitude of so many of the Negroes in the southern states; and in the sadistic insistence of the "white supremacists" in declaring that their will must be imposed irrespective of rights of other citizens. This claim of "white supremacy," while fantastic and without foundation, is really believed by them for we have had repeated declarations from leading politicians and governors of this state and other states declaring that "white supremacy" will be endangered by the abolition of segregation. There are present threats, including those of the present Governor of this state, going to the extent of saying that all public education may be abandoned if the courts should grant true equality in educational facilities....

We now come to the cases that, in my opinion, definitely and conclusively establish the doctrine that separation and segregation according to race is a violation of the Fourteenth Amendment.... In the instant case, the plaintiffs produced a large number of witnesses. It is significant that the defendants brought but two. These last two were not trained educators. One was an official of the Clarendon schools who said that the school system needed improvement and that the school officials were hopeful and expectant of obtaining money from State funds to improve all facilities. The other witness, significantly named Crow, has been recently employed by a commission just established which, it is proposed, will supervise educational facilities in the State and will handle monies if, as and when the same are received sometime in the future. Mr. Crow did not testify as an expert on education although he stated flatly that he believed in separation of the races and that he heard a number of other people say so, including some Negroes, but he was unable to mention any of their names. Mr. Crow explained what was likely and liable to happen under the 1951 State Educational Act to which frequent reference was made in argument on behalf of the defense....

On the other hand, the plaintiffs brought many witnesses, some of them of national reputation in various educational fields. It is unnecessary for me to review or analyze their testimony. But they who had made studies of education and its effect upon children, starting with the lowest grades and studying them up through and into high school, unequivocally testified that aside from inequality in housing appliances and equipment, the mere fact of segregation, itself, had a deleterious and warping effect upon the minds of children. These witnesses testified as to their study and researches and their actual tests with children of varying ages and they showed that the humiliation and disgrace of being set aside and segregated as unfit to associate with others of different color had an evil and ineradicable effect upon the mental processes of our young which would remain with them and deform their view on life until and throughout their maturity. This applies to white as well as Negro children. These witnesses testified from actual study and tests in various parts of the country, including tests in the actual Clarendon School district under consideration. They showed beyond a doubt that the evils of segregation and color prejudice come from early training. And from their testimony as well as from common experience and knowledge and from our own reasoning we must unavoidably come to the conclusion that racial prejudice is something that is acquired and that that acquiring is in early childhood. When do we get our first ideas of religion, nationality and the other basic ideologies? The vast number of individuals follow religious and political groups because of their childhood training. And it is difficult and nearly impossible to change and eradicate these early prejudices, however strong may be the appeal to reason. There is absolutely no reasonable explanation for racial prejudice. It is all caused by unreasoning emotional reactions and these are gained in early childhood. Let the little child's mind be poisoned by prejudice of this kind and it is practically impossible to ever remove these impressions however many years he may have of teaching by philosophers, religious leaders or patriotic citizens. If segregation is wrong then the place to stop it is in the first grade and not in graduate colleges.

From their testimony, it was clearly apparent, as it should be to any thoughtful person, irrespective of having such expert testimony, that segregation in education can never produce equality and that it is an evil that must be eradicated. This case presents the matter clearly for adjudication and I am of the opinion that all of the legal guideposts, expert testimony, common sense and reason point unerringly to the conclusion that the system of segregation in education adopted and practiced in the State of South Carolina must go and must go now.

Segregation is per se *inequality.*

As heretofore shown, the courts of this land have stricken down discrimination in higher education and have declared unequivocally that segregation is not equality. But these decisions have pruned away only the noxious fruits. Here in this case, we are asked to strike its very root. Or rather, to change the metaphor, we are asked to strike at the cause of infection and not merely at the symptoms of disease. And if the courts of this land are to render justice under the laws without fear or favor, justice for all men and all kinds of men, the time to do it is now and the place is in the elementary schools where our future citizens learn their first lesson to respect the dignity of the individual in a democracy....

For further reading, see *A Passion for Justice: J. Waties Waring and Civil Rights*, by Tinsley E. Yarbrough (Oxford University Press, 2001). The papers of Rev. Joseph Armstrong DeLaine are housed at the University of South Carolina. The DeLaine-Waring AME Church in Buffalo, New York continues to this day.

Judge Waring's many references to previous legal cases and decisions have been omitted, and it is hoped that students of law will research the complete document. Federal Supplement Volume 98 pages 529-567. The official cite is *Briggs v. Elliott*, 98 F. Supp. 529 (D.S.C. 1951).

4 Concerning the "Shoot Out" on October 10, 1955

Joseph A. DeLaine, Jr. is the eldest of Reverend Joseph A. and Mrs. Mattie DeLaine's three children. He and his brother, Brumit B. DeLaine, are on the Board of Directors of the Briggs-DeLaine-Pearson Foundation; and, with their sister, Dr. Ophelia DeLaine Gona, are active in the documentation of historic events involving their family. Mr. DeLaine, Jr. earned a B.A. degree from Lincoln University (Pennsylvania) in 1954, and pursued graduate studies at New York University. He is retired from Hoffmann La Roche, Incorporated, where he served in several management positions, including as Director of the Corporate Equal Employment Opportunity Department.

Mr. De Laine, Jr. was a member of the Fiftieth Anniversary Brown v. Board Presidential Commission and chair of the Briggs Descendants Reunion. He is a resident of Charlotte, North Carolina.

I. A Narrative
JOSEPH A. DELAINE, JR.

Mr. Web Eaddy and Mrs. Hattie Eaddy were members of Rev. DeLaine's church in Lake City, South Carolina. They also lived next door to the

61

parsonage and the church, and were contemporaries of my parents. Mrs. Eaddy was the aunt of Ossie Davis. The Eaddys' only child, Viola, was unable to provide any detailed information regarding the Lake City incident, since she was away in college at the time and only vaguely remembered hearing the details of what happened. My brother and sister were also away at school, and I myself was in the U.S. Army serving in Korea.

Based on information ascertained by me from Viola, my father's notes, my mother's recollections and those of a few other people, here is what apparently happened.

Four days before the "shoot out," the church where my father was a pastor—St. James Church in Lake City—was destroyed by arson. The next day he received an unsigned letter telling him to leave town or face the consequences. Around midnight of October 10, 1955, gunfire aimed at the parsonage where my parents resided, erupted from passing automobiles—the actions of the Ku Klux Klan. After the second round of automobiles and gunfire, Rev. DeLaine decided to return the fire. Mrs. DeLaine then also grabbed a gun to defend herself and her husband. Rev. DeLaine, fearful for my mother's life, insisted that she not become involved and urged her to leave by the rear door of the parsonage and seek refuge with neighbors. As Rev. DeLaine took Mrs. DeLaine to the back door to escape, he spotted figures in the back yard who were ready to shoot at the passing cars—Mr. Web Eaddy and his wife, Mrs. Hattie Eaddy. Once they identified themselves, Rev. DeLaine encouraged them not to become involved but to take Mrs. DeLaine into their home for safety. When the third round of gunfire erupted, Rev. DeLaine shot back and allegedly injured several individuals.

The night riders then quickly retreated and Rev. DeLaine pondered his next move. About twenty minutes later, the Negro policeman in Lake City appeared—the only black officer on the Lake City police force at that time. He told Rev. DeLaine that he was instructed to bring him to the police station, and that he feared they planned to kill DeLaine once he arrived there. The policeman said that he would return to the station and say that no one was found at the house. Rev. DeLaine immediately fled in his car without any communication with the Eaddys or his wife.

His odyssey took him to Florence, South Carolina, about thirty miles north of Lake City, where he found shelter with Attorney W. Bennett and his brother-in-law Mr. Guile (a next door neighbor) for the remainder of the night. Mr. Guile, president of the local county NAACP branch, was the husband of Mrs. Evelyn Guile, Mr. Bennett's sister. In 2006, Evelyn Guile was still living in the same location, and said she did not object to the use of their names.

Mr. Bennett went to Lake City at about 10A.M. the following day to find Mrs. DeLaine. When he arrived, the police were searching the parsonage. Attorney Bennett discreetly inquired among black people and was told that Mrs. DeLaine was being hidden in the Eaddy home next door. He was successful in securing Mrs. DeLaine and they left Lake City before the police were aware of their actions.

The two returned to Florence, picked up Rev. DeLaine, and proceeded to Charlotte, North Carolina, where the Reverend boarded a flight to Washington, D.C. Mrs. DeLaine remained with her brothers in Charlotte for the night and then went to her parents in Columbia, South Carolina. This move was in the hope of returning to Lake City for personal belongings and to plan the next steps.

In Washington, D.C., DeLaine's cousin Levi felt that the capitol city was too risky and that he should continue to New York. They left immediately by automobile for New York City.

I am quite certain that my father never saw the Eaddys after the night of the shoot out. It is possible that my mother may have seen one of them in later years. However, I feel confident that there was some form of communication between the Eaddys and my parents prior to their deaths. My brother, having relocated to Charlotte, North Carolina in about 1962, did have contact with their daughter, Viola. Upon my relocation to Charlotte in 1984, and through my brother, I also had periodic contact with Viola which lasted until her death in 2004.

II. Notes on the Aftermath
ALICE BERNSTEIN

Several days after Rev. DeLaine reached New York City as a fugitive, proceedings against him were dismissed in New York Felony Court by

Magistrate David L. Malbin, who stated that no extradition papers had ever been received from South Carolina. A newspaper reported that DeLaine, who described himself as a political fugitive, said the dismissal was an "example of true justice."

Among the Joseph Armstrong DeLaine papers, housed at the University of South Carolina in the South Caroliniana Library, is a letter to the Reverend from William J. Hayes, Executive Director of the Young Men's Civic Club in Lake City, written on October 24, 1955. In a passionate show of support, Mr. Hayes writes: "Many like episodes followed the one on the night of your departure. Many more Negroes were grief stricken and frightened out of their wits, but the BIG THREE (KKK) has not as of yet, taken us down. We plan to hold our heads higher now than ever, and if there is any information we can furnish you for any court situation, don't be afraid to let us know. We are with you and everything that you stood for....And like you, I stand ready to do as you have done...."

The following year, in a letter dated October 15, 1956, Rev. DeLaine's colleague Rev. E. E. Richburg in Summerton, SC wrote to DeLaine, then in Buffalo, New York, and enclosed a check towards the founding of the DeLaine-Waring AME Church. The letter lists the names of sixty-five contributors from Liberty Hill Church, who thank him "for everything you have done...and for the interest you still have in our welfare." It ends with the sentence: "God will make a way for you and your family for you have done no wrong, you have rendered an unselfish service to your community, county, state, and nation."

As the result of efforts begun in 1955 by Rev. F.C. James, pastor of Mount Pisgah AME Church in Sumter, and renewed by State Representative Alex Harvin III many years after DeLaine's death—Rev. DeLaine's name was cleared through a pardon from the South Carolina State Parole Board in 2000. This was followed by a celebration in Summerton.

In 2006, Rev. DeLaine was inducted into the South Carolina Education Hall of Honor at the Museum of Education, University of South Carolina.

5 Awarding Congressional Gold Medals

In 2004, the 108th Congress passed a bill, H.R. 3287, sponsored by Congressman James E. Clyburn (D-SC) in the House, and a similar bill sponsored by Senator Ernest Frederick "Fritz" Hollings (D-SC) in the Senate, issuing U.S. Congressional Gold Medals in honor of Rev. DeLaine, Harry and Eliza Briggs, and Levi Pearson.

Excerpts from the Congressional Record:
November 18, 2003 (House of Representatives)

AWARDING CONGRESSIONAL GOLD MEDALS
POSTHUMOUSLY ON BEHALF OF REVEREND JOSEPH A.
DeLAINE, HARRY AND ELIZA BRIGGS, AND LEVI PEARSON
IN RECOGNITION OF THEIR CONTRIBUTIONS TO *BROWN V.
BOARD OF EDUCATION*

The Clerk read as follows:

H.R. 3287

Be it enacted by the Senate and House of Representatives of the United States of America in Congress assembled,

SECTION 1. FINDINGS.

The Congress finds as follows:

(1) The Reverend Joseph Armstrong DeLaine, one of the true heroes of the civil rights struggle, led a crusade to break down barriers in education in South Carolina.

(2) The efforts of Reverend DeLaine led to the desegregation of public schools in the United States, but forever scarred his own life.

(3) In 1949, Joseph DeLaine, a minister and school principal, organized African American parents in Summerton, South Carolina, to petition the school board for a bus for black students, who had to walk up to ten miles through corn and cotton fields to attend a segregated school, while the white children in the school district rode to and from school in nice clean buses.

(4) In 1950, these same parents, including Harry and Eliza Briggs, sued to end public school segregation in *Briggs et al. v. Elliott et al.*, one of five cases that collectively led to the landmark 1954 Supreme Court decision of *Brown et al. v. Board of Education of Topeka et al.*

(5) Because of his participation in the desegregation movement, Reverend DeLaine was subjected to repeated acts of domestic terror in which—

(A) he, along with two sisters and a niece, lost their jobs;

(B) he fought off an angry mob;

(C) he received frequent death threats; and

(D) his church and his home were burned to the ground.

(6) In October 1955, after Reverend DeLaine relocated to Florence County in South Carolina, shots were fired at the DeLaine home, and because Reverend DeLaine fired back to mark the car, he was charged with assault and battery with intent to kill.

(7) The shooting incident drove him from South Carolina to Buffalo, New York, where he organized an African Methodist Episcopal Church.

(8) Believing that he would not be treated fairly by the South Carolina judicial system if he returned to South Carolina, Reverend DeLaine told the Federal Bureau of Investigation, "I am not running from justice but injustice," and it was not until 2000 (twenty-six years after his death and forty-five years after the incident) that Reverend DeLaine was cleared of all charges relating to the October 1955 incident.

(9) Reverend DeLaine was a humble and fearless man who showed the Nation that all people, regardless of the color of their skin, deserve a first-rate education, a lesson from which the Nation has benefited immeasurably.

(10) Reverend DeLaine deserves rightful recognition for the suffering that he and his family endured to teach the Nation one of the great civil rights lessons of the last century.

(11) Like the Reverend DeLaine and Harry and Eliza Briggs, Levi Pearson was an integral participant in the struggle to equalize the educational experiences of white and black students in South Carolina.

(12) Levi Pearson, with the assistance of Reverend Joseph DeLaine, filed a lawsuit against the Clarendon County School District to protest the inequitable treatment of black children.

(13) As a result of his lawsuit, Levi Pearson also suffered from acts of domestic terror, such as the time gun shots were fired into his home, as well as economic consequences: local banks refused to provide him with credit to purchase farming materials and area farmers refused to lend him equipment.

(14) Although his case was ultimately dismissed on a technicality, Levi Pearson's courage to stand up for equalized treatment and funding for black students served as the catalyst for further attempts to desegregate South Carolina schools, as he continued to fight against segregation practices and became President of Clarendon County Chapter of the NAACP.

(15) When Levi Pearson's litigation efforts to obtain equalized treatment and funding for black students were stymied, Harry and Eliza Briggs, a service station attendant and a maid, continued to fight for not only equalized treatment of all children but desegregated schools as well.

(16) As with Reverend DeLaine and Levi Pearson, the family of Harry and Eliza Briggs suffered consequences for their efforts: Harry and Eliza both were fired from their jobs and forced to move their family to Florida.

(17) Although they and their family suffered tremendously, Harry and Eliza Briggs were also pioneers leading the effort to desegregate America's public schools.

SECTION 2. CONGRESSIONAL GOLD MEDAL.

(a) Presentation Authorized. —In recognition of the contributions of Reverend Joseph A. DeLaine, Harry and Eliza Briggs, and Levi Pearson to the Nation as pioneers in the effort to desegregate public schools that led directly to the landmark desegregation case of *Brown et al. v. the Board of Education of Topeka et al.*, the Speaker of the House of Representatives and the President Pro Tempore of the Senate shall make appropriate arrangements for the presentation, on behalf of the Congress, of a gold medal of appropriate design, to Joseph DeLaine, Jr., as next of kin of Reverend Joseph A. DeLaine, and to the next of kin or other personal representative of Harry and Eliza Briggs and of Levi Pearson.

(b) Design and Striking. —For the purposes of the awards referred to in subsection (a), the Secretary of the Treasury (hereafter in this Act referred to as the "Secretary") shall strike three gold medals with suitable emblems, devices, and inscriptions, to be determined by the Secretary....

The following are remarks from Congressman James E. Clyburn (D-SC) of the Sixth District.

Mr. CLYBURN. It is very difficult to find proper words to convey to the 298 cosponsors of this bill my appreciation of the bipartisan support and genuine courtesies extended to me throughout this effort.

Mr. Speaker, I am also grateful to Senator Fritz Hollings for his sponsorship of similar legislation in the other body and his ninety-nine colleagues who gave his bill a unanimous vote. I am hopeful this body will do likewise.

Mr. Speaker, as we approach the fiftieth anniversary of *Brown v. Board of Education of Topeka, Kansas,* it is indeed an honor to stand in the Halls of the United States House of Representatives to commemorate the dedication and courage of four South Carolinians who initiated the effort to desegregate public school education in South Carolina and the Nation.

Reverend Joseph Armstrong DeLaine organized the original 106 petitioners, eighteen of whom and two others made up the original twenty plaintiffs in *Briggs v. Elliott,* the first of the five cases that were merged and became *Brown v. Board of Education of Topeka, Kansas.* I now submit the names of all of those petitioners into the Record of these proceedings this evening.

Briggs v. Elliott

The petition was submitted on November 11, 1949 (see Figure 1, pp. 74-75). South Carolinians who signed a petition to the Board of Trustees for Clarendon County School District No. 22 demanding equal educational opportunities for African Americans.

At the time of their petition, black children in Clarendon County were walking nine miles each way to school, and all they petitioned for was a school bus. When their request for a bus was denied, they sought relief in the courts. Reverend DeLaine was harassed by the Ku Klux Klan and several attempts were made on his life....

In 1971, Governor John C. West received a letter from Reverend

DeLaine advising that his health was failing and requesting that he be allowed to return to South Carolina where he wished to be buried. Governor West tasked me with the responsibility of getting it done. We failed, because one of the men who signed the arrest warrant refused the Governor's and law enforcement officials' requests that he drop the charges. In 2000, the South Carolina legislature cleared Reverend DeLaine's record, but much too late to honor his request. Reverend DeLaine died in 1974 and is buried in Charlotte, North Carolina.

Levi Pearson was a small Clarendon County farmer. He responded to Reverend DeLaine's request and sued the school district on behalf of his three children who were walking those nine miles to school each day. His decision was met with dire consequences. The local bank refused to provide him credit to purchase farming equipment and other farmers refused to lend him any equipment. Shots were fired into his home and he was ostracized by his neighbors. Despite these actions, Pearson continued with his suit. But in 1948, the United States District Court dismissed Pearson's suit, finding that although his farm was partially in Clarendon School District One, his house was situated in Clarendon School District Two; and therefore he had no standing. Although his legal case was dismissed, Pearson continued to fight against segregation and later became president of the local NAACP chapter. In spite of extreme hardships, he never left his land.

Harry Briggs, a service station attendant, and his wife, Eliza, a maid at a local motel, took up the cause. As did Levi Pearson and Reverend DeLaine, they suffered inhumane consequences for their actions. They were fired from their jobs but they persevered, and as is often said, the rest is history. Because he was blackballed in South Carolina and could not find employment, Harry moved to Florida where he lived out his productive life. Unlike Reverend DeLaine, he returned to South Carolina and is buried in his native soil.

Every year on the Friday evening nearest May 17, the South Carolina conference of branches of the NAACP holds its annual Freedom Fund dinner in honor of the Briggs petitioners. And ever since I have been a Member of this body, pictures of Mrs. DeLaine and other principals in the case have been prominently displayed on a wall of my office.

Mr. Speaker, if not for the personal sacrifices of those like Reverend

DeLaine, Mr. Pearson, the Briggses and many others known and unknown, I and others like me may have never experienced membership in this body. This bill reminds us that it is the actions of a preacher and educator, a farmer, a gas station attendant, and a motel maid that initiated the efforts that changed American society forever. I hope that our actions here tonight remind all Americans that it is not our station in life that makes us worthy of honor and recognition, but our commitment to the principles and pursuit of the promise that all men are created equal, that they are endowed by their Creator with certain unalienable rights, that among these are life, liberty, and the pursuit of happiness....

The following are remarks from U.S. Representative John Spratt (D-SC) of the Fifth District.

Mr. SPRATT. Mr. Speaker, I rise in proud support of H.R. 3287, which honors four South Carolina heroes.... I have the same story to tell that the gentleman from South Carolina (Mr. Clyburn) just told, but I cannot possibly tell it with the same empathy that he related it, so I will not rehearse the facts that we have just heard, which are stirring. I will enter those for the Record.

Let me simply say that, Mr. Speaker, I have lived all my life in South Carolina. I can imagine the resistance and intimidation that Joseph DeLaine and Levi Pearson and Harry and Eliza Briggs faced. These brave Americans stood up for justice, and for their courage they paid a heavy price. Today we remember Dr. Martin Luther King and Thurgood Marshall, and we should. They were the giants of the civil rights movement. But without brave pioneers, foot soldiers like Joseph A. DeLaine, Levi Pearson, and Harry and Eliza Briggs, our schools would not have been desegregated in 1954. The Civil Rights Act of 1964 and 1965 may have been passed but not in those years. They sparked those events....

In 1949-50, there were 6,531 black students enrolled in the Clarendon County public schools and 2,375 whites. The schools were separate and unequal. Clarendon County that year spent $179.00 per white student and $43.00 per black student. Reverend Joseph DeLaine was a teacher in

Clarendon County. He attended a statewide meeting of the NAACP and heard the president decry segregation and lay down a challenge saying, "No teacher or preacher in South Carolina has the courage to find a plaintiff who will test the legality of discriminatory bus transportation." The Reverend DeLaine was moved to action. He went to the Clarendon County School Board to ask for a bus to carry children to and from Scotts Branch High School.

He pointed out that bus service was available to white students at other county schools, and asked simply for the same bus service for black students attending Scotts Branch. When he was turned down, he appealed to the State Superintendent of Education in Columbia and the U.S. Attorney General, all to no avail....

Undaunted, Reverend DeLaine, worked with the NAACP to draft a new petition to the State Board of Education seeking not just school buses, but educational equality across the board for all black students in Clarendon County. A petition with the necessary signatures was presented to the board.... The state school board refused to act.

Reverend DeLaine then sought the assistance of the NAACP Legal Defense Fund, and in particular a lawyer by the name of Harold Boulware in Columbia. Boulware, with the assistance of Thurgood Marshall, took the case and filed a new suit, *Briggs v. Elliott*, seeking equal educational opportunities for all black students in Clarendon County...eventually consolidated with four other cases, the first of which was *Brown v. Board of Education of Topeka, Kansas*.

Reverend DeLaine was in the Supreme Court's courtroom for the argument of *Brown v. Board of Education*. A reporter quoted him as saying: "There were times when I thought I would go out of my mind because of this case, but if I had to do it again, I would. I feel it was worth it. I have a feeling that the Supreme Court is going to end segregation."

He was not only brave but prescient.

Briggs v. Elliott

The South Carolinians who signed a petition to the Board of Trustees for Clarendon County School District No. 22 demanding equal educational opportunities for African Americans.

Waiting to get into the courtroom of the U.S. Superme Court.
(Library of Congress photo.)

Figure 1

Briggs v. Elliott Petition Signatures
The petition was submitted on November 11, 1949.

1. Harry Briggs*
2. Eliza Briggs
3. Harry Briggs, Jr.
4. Thomas Lee Briggs
5. Katherine Briggs
6. Thomas Gamble
7. Henry Brown
8. Thelma Brown
9. Vera Brown
10. Beatrice Brown
11. Willie Brown
12. Marian Brown
13. Ethel Mae Brown
14. Howard Brown
15. James Brown
16. Theola Brown
17. Thomas Brown
18. Euralia Brown
19. Joe Morris Brown
20. Onetha Bennett*
21. Hercules Bennett
22. Hilton Bennett
23. William Gibson
24. Annie Gibson*
25. William Gibson Jr.

26. Maxine Gibson
27. Harold Gibson
28. Robert Georgia*
29. Carrie Georgia
30. Charlie Georgia
31. Jervine Georgia
32. Gladys Hilton
33. Joseph Hilton
34. Lila Mae Huggins
35. Celestine Huggins
36. Juanita Huggins
37. Gussie Hilton
38. Roosevelt Hilton
39. Thomas Johnson
40. Blanche E. Johnson
41. Lillie Eva Johnson
42. Rubie Lee Johnson
43. Betty J. Johnson
44. Bobby M. Johnson
45. Preston Johnson Jr.
46. Susan Lawson*
47. Raymond Lawson
48. Eddie Lee Lawson
49. Susan Ann Lawson
50. Frederick Oliver*

---

51. Willie Oliver
52. Mary Oliver*
53. Mose Oliver*
54. Leroy Oliver
55. Mitchel Oliver
56. Bennie Parson Jr.*
57. Plummie Parson
58. Celestine Parson
59. Edward Ragin*
60. Sarah Ragin
61. Shirley Ragin
62. Deloris Ragin
63. Hazel Ragin*
64. Zelia Ragin
65. Sarah Ellen Ragin
66. Rebecca Ragin
67. Mable Ragin
68. William Ragin*
69. Glen Ragin
70. Luchrisher Richardson*
71. Elane Richardson
72. Emanuel Richardson
73. Rebecca Richburg*
74. Rebecca I. Richburg
75. E.E. Richburg
76. Albert Richburg
77. Lee Johnson
78. Bessie Johnson
79. Morgan Johnson
80. Samuel Gary Johnson
81. Lee Richardson*
82. James Richardson
83. Charles Richardson
84. Annie L. Richardson
85. Dorothy Richardson
86. Jackson Richardson
87. Mary O. Lawson
88. Francis Lawson
89. Bennie Lee Lawson
90. Mary Oliver
91. Daisy Oliver
92. Louis Oliver Jr.
93. Esther F. Singleton
94. Janie Fludde
95. Henry Scott*
96. Mary Scott
97. Irene Scott
98. Willie M. Stukes*
99. Gardenia Stukes
100. Willie M. Stukes Jr.
101. Gardenia Stukes
102. Louis W. Stukes
103. Gabriel Tyndal*
104. Annie Tyndal
105. Mary L. Bennett
106. Lillian Bennett

* Indicates those who served as named plaintiffs in the case of *Briggs v. Elliott*. Plaintiffs also included James H. Bennett and G. H. Henry.

6 Racism Can End
ELLEN REISS

Ellen Reiss is the Class Chairman of Aesthetic Realism, appointed by Eli Siegel. A critic and poet, she teaches the professional classes for Aesthetic Realism Consultants and Associates, as well as the course "The Aesthetic Realism Explanation of Poetry," at the Aesthetic Realism Foundation. Prior to becoming Class Chairman, she taught in the English departments of Hunter College and Queens College of the City University of New York.

She is co-author, with Martha Baird, of the Williams-Siegel Documentary *(Definition Press), and wrote the Introductions to* Children's Guide to Parents & Other Matters, *by Eli Siegel (Definition Press), and* Quintillions, *by Robert Clairmont (American Sunbeam Publisher). She is the editor of the international periodical* The Right of Aesthetic Realism to Be Known, *where her commentaries on current events, literature, history, and the human self appear biweekly. The following is reprinted from her commentary in issue #1264 (June 25, 1997).*

Racism Can End

In his 1951 lecture *Aesthetic Realism as Thought*, Eli Siegel shows something never seen before: thought, emotions, and art have a basis in common. That basis

76

is in the Aesthetic Realism principle, stated by him: "The world, art, and self explain each other: each is the aesthetic oneness of opposites."

For example, every instance of thought—from arithmetic, to Beethoven's thought as he composed his Fifth Symphony, to a woman's thought about love—is a dealing with the sameness and difference of reality. For the sameness and difference of things is present in quantities, notes, and our being affected by someone who has the temerity to be *not us.* How accurately and deeply and richly we see sameness and difference is how good our thought is.

The fact that this matter is the same as pulsing, hoping, and often agonized life, can be seen through something reported in the *New York Times* on June 11. Under the headline "New Survey Shows Americans Pessimistic on Race Relations," Steven A. Holmes writes that according to a Gallup poll "a majority of Americans are pessimistic that blacks and whites will ever learn to get along."

I am completely sure that racism can end, through the study of Aesthetic Realism. It is the knowledge through which white people and black people—as they see one another on the street, in a classroom, in the office—can have feelings about each other that are alive with kindness and respect.

Where Prejudice Begins

The big thing people have not known about racial prejudice is that it does not begin with race. It begins with the world itself, and how one sees the world. Race will never be understood and racial prejudice will not end until people can learn the following from Aesthetic Realism: (1) Race is an aspect of the aesthetic structure, the sameness-and-difference structure, of the world. This structure is what we see as we see two different things, ocean and sky, inextricably part of one horizon; as different words join together to make one sentence; as a tree's trunk and leaves are different yet *for* each other, sweetly and powerfully coherent with each other. Whenever, Mr. Siegel showed, we see difference and sameness as one, we see beauty. (2) No person would be against people of a different race if that person were not against the biggest thing different from him: *the world.*

Let us take a girl we can call Heather Norris, born in Vermont fifteen years ago. Aesthetic Realism explains that while Heather was born to particular parents, she was born, like every child, into the whole world other than

77

herself—of objects and history and sun and money and words and human beings. Mr. Siegel explained that there is a fight within every person concerning that reality different from oneself. It is the fight between *respect* and *contempt*.

The purpose of Heather's life—what she, as a tiny baby lying in a Vermont crib, was born for—was to respect the world, like it. That means, to feel that things and people in all their difference from her were related to her too: they could add to her, make her more herself through her wanting to know and value them. But within Heather and all of us there was and is another possibility: the false, hurtful dealing with sameness and difference, which is *contempt*. Mr. Siegel described contempt as the "disposition in every person to think he will be for himself by making less of the outside world."

She Did Not Like the World

Heather was bewildered by the world she met. Her parents, being human, confused her. They could buy her presents and tell her she was gorgeous, brilliant, "the most special girl in the world," and then sometimes they could seem not interested in her at all. Further, she came to feel her parents were stupid for praising her so lavishly and that other people were cold and mean for not doing so. She disliked the world because she saw some bad things in it: she saw selfishness in people, and her keen ears discerned hypocrisy. But she also disliked the world for being complicated, for confusing her, for having so many different things and happenings and people that she couldn't understand fast and that didn't give her her way.

By the time she was eight, this representative person was in a contest with the world different from her—that contest which is contempt. She went after feeling sure and important through feeling other things were deeply separate from her, that the reality within herself was warmer, profounder, more precious than the reality outside her. She did not see the other children in her third grade class as having the insides she had—the full range of feelings, the thoughts in bed at night—even though she could play energetically with those children and giggle with them. There was a big desire in Heather—a representative, ordinary, terrible desire, simmering along hour by hour—to punish the world, beat it out, to feel she mattered by showing that other things *didn't* matter, weren't good enough for her. She liked making fun of her teacher with her friends. She felt like she was important then—that someone who had made her feel she needed to learn things wasn't as good as she was.

She Became a Racist

When Heather saw a girl whose skin was a color different from hers, she, without knowing it, was seeing someone who vividly embodied the *world* as different from her, a world she wanted to defeat. Heather seized the opportunity to despise this girl and others with that different skin color. The feeling of revulsion and superiority she had as to them was the fake, horrible, yet ferociously desired victory of contempt: of feeling she was somebody just because she could look down on what was different.

Heather heard someone use a crude, demeaning word about a person of another race. That word appealed to her. And the first time she used it— toward a girl in her class—she felt a thrill. It was the thrill of feeling that in one swift utterance she had put in its place not only a person but the world different from her. She could get to quick sureness by defeating what was other than herself: by making difference—in the form of an eight-year-old black girl— look low and ridiculous through two sneering syllables. The sureness, being fake, didn't last; and the contempt, the untruth, it was based on made Heather feel often deeply nervous and dreary. But she relished those moments of swift, sneering, conquering sureness and kept going after them.

The horrible way Heather saw black people continued because her desire to have contempt for a world not herself continued. Now she is fifteen. With some friends, she has spray-painted ugly words on a church attended by African Americans in her town.

Meanwhile, Heather's contempt for people of another race had as a prerequisite for its existence a dislike of people as such. Most persons are like her: they see people not as deeply adding to them but as means to be important, praised, superior. And (as I have said in previous TROs) profit economics, with its horrible way of seeing people, has led to an increase of racism in America. Men and women worry about jobs and money, and rightly hate being seen by a boss in terms of how much profit they can produce for him. But they wrongly use their anger to dislike the world itself; and they try to even the score through looking down on persons standing for that world different from them.

What Must Replace Racism

Aesthetic Realism shows—greatly, efficiently, kindly shows—that for racism to end we have to be against the thing it begins with: contempt for the world itself. Further, racism won't be effectively done away with unless it is replaced with something that has terrific power. What needs to replace it is not the feeling that the difference of another person is somehow tolerable. What is necessary is the seeing and feeling that the relation of sameness and difference between ourselves and that other person is *beautiful.* People need to feel, with feeling both intimately personal and large, that difference of race is like the difference to be found in music: two notes are different, but they are in behalf of the same melody; they complete each other; each needs the other to be expressed richly, to be fully itself.

It is possible for millions of men, women, and children to have an emotion about race that is like an art emotion. And it is necessary. It will happen when America is studying Aesthetic Realism.

To show in one more way the art feeling—the only practical and just feeling—Americans can have about race, I quote a 1970 poem by Eli Siegel. It has, with its rich music, his beautiful logic and tenderness:

> *Only Later; or, The First Line*
> I heard a Negro child crying
> And it sounded so much like a white child
> It was only later
> I found out what I said
> In my first line.

7 The Aesthetic Realism Teaching Method: Two Examples

Printed here are accounts by two New York City educators of the lessons they have taught using the Aesthetic Realism Teaching Method. This method succeeds at every grade level and in the teaching of every subject. In his tribute to Eli Siegel, published July 26, 2002, in the U.S. Congressional Record, Elijah E. Cummings, then Chair of the Congressional Black Caucus, noted that the Aesthetic Realism Teaching Method "has been tremendously successful" and that it is "an effective tool to stop racism and promote tolerance; because it enables people of all races to see others with respect and kindness."

At the method's basis are the following Aesthetic Realism principles:

1. *"The purpose of education is to like the world through knowing it."*

2. *The greatest interference to learning is contempt, "the lessening of what is different from oneself as a means of self-increase as one sees it."*

3. *"The world, art, and self explain each other: each is the aesthetic oneness of opposites."*

In the accounts that follow, the names of students have been changed.

I.

Monique Michael was born in Port-au-Prince, Haiti. *A graduate of Hunter College, she studied with historian John Henrik Clarke and majored in Black and Puerto Rican Studies. An elementary school educator since 1992, she has presented seminar papers and conducted workshops describing the success of the Aesthetic Realism Teaching Method, including at educational conferences of the National Council of Teachers of English and the National Science Teachers Association. She currently works as a Reading Recovery/Academic Intervention teacher at P.S. 184 on New York's Lower East Side, and is the author of the groundbreaking article "Children Learn to Read through the Aesthetic Realism Teaching Method." She and her husband, maritime captain and photographer Allan Michael, have written articles on Aesthetic Realism as the knowledge that can end racism, which have appeared widely.*

First Grade Children Learn and Become Kinder
MONIQUE MICHAEL

It moves me very much to be able to say that racism is not inevitable. Because the philosopher Eli Siegel understood the cause of racism, people of different backgrounds can learn to honestly, and warmly, respect each other and feel proud doing so. Both my personal life and my professional life using the Aesthetic Realism teaching method in New York City classrooms for fifteen years—six in East Harlem—are evidence for this.

From an early age I was encouraged to be prejudiced. As a mixed person born into Haitian society, I looked down on my African ancestry. I got the message that being white was far superior to being black. For instance, I was told that I should not marry a black man because my family had to become lighter rather than darker as the generations went on. For most of my life I felt I was better that anyone who was darker skinned and poorer than my family.

I had no idea that this racist attitude hurt me and made me feel I did not know where I belonged, until I began to study Aesthetic Realism. Because of what I learned, I was able to welcome and be proud of both my African and European ancestries and I finally felt like an integrity.

The Aesthetic Realism Teaching Method is urgently needed because it opposes the contempt for the world that is at the basis of racism, and encourages a new respect for the difference that is in the world and for people. It states that the purpose of education is to like the world through knowing it; and shows that the reason the world can be liked is that it has a sensible, beautiful structure which is related to us: it is a oneness of opposites. This structure is in every person and every subject of the curriculum.

Sameness and Difference in Birds

As an example, I'll describe a first grade life science lesson on birds, illustrating animal adaptations, a concept that is part of the New York City science curriculum for the elementary grades. As I taught this lesson using the Aesthetic Realism method, students (1) were encouraged to know and like the world more as they saw the beauty of the sameness and difference of birds, and (2) were able to see the cause of racism and have it opposed in themselves.

I began by telling my students that there are thousands of different kinds of birds in the world. As I showed them pictures of a toucan, an owl, a humming bird, and ducks, they were surprised by the diversity they saw. I asked, "What makes them all birds?" "Feathers, wings," they answered. "What makes them all different?" "Their colors, size, feet, songs!" the children called out with excitement.

We looked closely at how the owls and the ducks are made. "What do you notice about the duck's and owl's eyes that makes them very different?" They saw that the owl had big eyes which faced forward while the duck's eyes were smaller and placed on the side of its head. "Why do you think there is this difference?" I asked. We learned that owls have to see at night as they search for prey, and ducks have to be able to see all around them.

As we looked at why these birds' feet are different, I asked, "Where have you seen ducks?" and "Where have you seen owls?" The webbed feet of the ducks enable them to swim, while the owls' individual toes and sharp claws make it possible for them to perch on trees. "Did the world make these birds different so they could best fit with the world around them?" "Yes!" the children answered. "Does this fact show that the world had a kind purpose in making birds different? As you see different birds and learn about how and why they are the same and different, is it very exciting?" The children loved learning this—and they answered a resounding "no" to the question, "Would you like the world more and find it more interesting if there existed only one type of bird?"

We Look at People

Then I told my students what I learned in anthropology classes taught by Aesthetic Realism consultant and anthropologist Dr. Arnold Perey—that our physical differences exist for the same kind reason that birds are different from each other—to have us fit better with the world. The differences among us are much, much less than the differences of those birds: we're more like variations of the same kind of bird. But certain physical differences come from the *big need we all have in common:* to put together the opposites of *self* and *world.* Humankind began in Africa, where people were dark so that they could be protected from the sun. As people moved to where it was colder, they grew longer hair to stay warm and their skins became lighter. People from many parts of Asia have an extra fold of skin on their eyes and flatter faces because they once lived where it was cold and windy: the extra skin protected their eyes and the flatter shape of their faces protected their noses from getting frostbitten.

I asked, "Is there something beautiful that you can respect about why we look different? Did the world make us look different for a beautiful reason: so our selves and the world could get along? When we use the fact that people look different from us to feel we are better than they are, that we are big and they are less, we are having contempt. This is what makes people mean to each other, call each other names; and when we have contempt we feel ashamed inside."

Through this lesson children see the beauty of sameness and difference in birds and in human beings—which encourages them to respect both more.

And the ugliest thing in humanity, contempt, which is at the root of the prejudice many of my students experience and also have for others, is opposed. As a result of this and other lessons based on the Aesthetic Realism method, I have seen children who continually fought with each other stop doing so and become much more thoughtful—both about each other and the subjects we're studying. They learn, and retain what they learn. For example, there's Nellie, who changed so much that she told me that now she wanted "to learn about the world all the time." There's Raphael, who said with excitement, "Now I really like school!" There's the parent who said about the lesson just described, "This is so important. It should be taught in all the schools."

It is the pride of my life that I am able, through the kind and scientific principles of the Aesthetic Realism teaching method, to bring out in my students their desire to know the world and to respect people.

II.

Barbara McClung, a New York City teacher and Aesthetic Realism Associate, has taught in public schools since 1984, on both the elementary and junior high school levels. Mrs. McClung has conducted workshops on the success of the Aesthetic Realism Teaching Method, at conferences in New York, New Jersey, and Maryland, including for the National Council of Teachers of English and the National Science Teachers Association. With Aesthetic Realism consultant and Emmy Award-winning filmmaker Ken Kimmelman, she has presented a children's workshop, "The Heart Knows Better: Changing Prejudice to Kindness," at schools and libraries. And with Aesthetic Realism consultant Devorah Tarrow, she conducts the interactive event for adults and children "Harriet Tubman, the Underground Railroad, and How Aesthetic Realism Explains the Cause of Slavery."

A Science Class Combats Prejudice
BARBARA MCCLUNG

I have seen with my own eyes how prejudice ends when students learn what Eli Siegel explained. Their deepest hope, and the purpose of all education, is *to like the world through knowing it.* This hope is met when young people see through the subjects they study that the world has a structure—*the oneness of opposites*—which can be honestly respected; and that this same structure of opposites is in every person no matter what his or her accent or ethnic background! As students see that the world can be liked because it is made well, they don't want to hurt people standing for it—they want to learn about it!

I'll tell about a science class I taught at JHS 56 on Manhattan's Lower East Side. The young people in this class represent diverse cultures (African American, Latino, and Asian) and have experienced the brutality of prejudice. As in other inner-city schools, they also look at each other with suspicion and enmity. The students at JHS 56M are terrifically hurt by worry about money, rent, and whether their parents will hold on to their jobs. For anyone to have to be concerned about having enough food is barbaric, and is due to the contempt at the basis of our failed economy.

At the beginning of the year, the seventh grade students I met were excited to be in a new school; but there was also a desire in them to mock, and insult each other. For instance, Justine Nichols seemed always ready for a fight and would get into confrontations with other students and even teachers. Ricky Olivera was suspicious, keeping himself apart, then suddenly telling another student to leave him alone. Often he didn't come to school.

I am enormously fortunate to have learned about contempt in myself. I used growing up in a middle class town in Connecticut to feel superior to children who lived in poorer areas. I also felt I was essentially different from *everybody*; and my contempt made me feel ashamed and cold. If I had not heard criticism from Aesthetic Realism, teaching in a classroom at all, to say nothing of a New York City classroom, would have been impossible for me. Never did I dream that I would have the deep feelings for the students I teach that I do today.

The Nervous System is Anti-Prejudice

In a series of lessons on the nervous system, my students learned that every person's body (no matter what our skin color) is made to know the world. We began to see that the nervous system is a beautiful oneness of inside and outside, being affected and affecting, or, as Mr. Siegel writes, "perceiving and responding."

Young people and others are troubled by the way they perceive and respond, are affected and affect. I have seen students look blank and sit dully, then suddenly lash out. Seeing how our nervous system puts these opposites together was thrilling. We learned that it is a network of 12 billion cells that links together all parts of the body, and every nerve cell, or neuron, is made in order to perceive messages and respond or act on them. At one end of the neuron are dendrites—fingerlike branches that receive incoming impulses. The impulse or message travels into the cell body and along the axon, which relays the message to the next neuron. And a nerve can send up to a thousand impulses a second!

These facts have been in textbooks for years, but have not done a thing to stop prejudice. However, as my students saw through the Aesthetic Realism method that the structure of the world itself—the oneness of such opposites as perceiving and responding, inside and outside, great speed and tremendous precision—is in the nervous system of every person, they began to look at each other differently: with respect and a deep friendliness! They also wanted to learn—and learned successfully.

We Need What Is Different from Us

There are two aspects to the nervous system: the central nervous system, consisting of the brain and spinal cord, where decisions are made as to what the body should do; and the peripheral nervous system, which consists of sensory and motor neurons extending from the brain and spinal cord throughout the body. Our brain depends on the peripheral nerves to bring it information.

I asked the class, "Suppose the brain said, 'I'm such a superior organ, I don't need these other nerves—they're so inferior to me!' Would the brain be able to do its job?" "No!" said Juan Aguilera. "You could be hurting yourself and wouldn't even know it," said Susan Lin. And if the peripheral nervous system looked down on and didn't have anything to do with the central nervous system? "There'd be messages all over the place, but no one to tell them what to do," said Neftali Diaz. And Linus Reed shouted, "You wouldn't be able to move!" I asked the class what would happen if the nervous system had contempt for what was outside the body and couldn't be affected by the taste of hot chocolate, by a kiss, or a good book. "We would be dead," said Marco Ortega soberly. And Janice Goodard said, "We'd be numb and dumb!"

This lesson made for greater kindness in my students–including among those of different ethnic backgrounds. They wrote deeply about how they need the world different from them—laws, language, food, and each other—to be who they are. Ricky Olivera, who had been so separate, wrote, "You need people and things to be all you can be, to encourage you to be the best that you can be in life." Ricky began coming to school regularly, doing assignments, and began to have friends like Jason McGee, a boy he once saw as so different from himself and would never speak to!

Justine Nichols, instead of looking for fights, now got along with her classmates and teachers. She wrote: "I used to think no one was like me, that they were stupid. But now I like meeting new people and new things."

Andy Reynolds said: "This class made me respect the world more. It has made me have respect for people." And Jamie Wang agreed: "I have learned that no matter how you look on the outside, on the inside you're the same. All people have a mind, a heart, and feelings."

I want every teacher to know of this practical, powerful teaching method so the children of America can have the education they deserve.

8 Remarks on "Speaking Freely"
OSSIE DAVIS

My commitment to the struggle began when I was a boy in Waycross, Georgia. My parents were involved in trying to get schooling for us, trying to get votes, and trying to do things that would better the lot of black people.

At the high school that I went to, our teachers felt strongly about the question of freedom, and they used to instill in us that everything we did—the way we spelled a word, the way we walked down the street—had some resonance in the outer community. And they spoke to the condition of black people. So, you mustn't do anything to cast aspersion on black people.

On the other hand, the white community would listen to us as we sang, or they would watch us as we danced. So our arts, even in those days, were ways of making a statement to the community about who we were. I grew up in those surroundings; it was a natural part of my training as a human being. Ruby grew up in Harlem, but her mother here in New York was roughly involved in the same kind of thing. She was a member of the NAACP, trying to get better schools, concerned about what was happening in the outer world.

When I came back from World War II—this was before I met Ruby— already the response to the returning black soldier was of grave concern to the black community. Black soldiers were being lynched; a soldier in North

Carolina had his eyes gouged out, Isaac Woodward. And two soldiers in Georgia [George Dorsey and Roger Malcom] walking with their wives were killed by the Ku Klux Klan. [Their wives, one seven months pregnant, were also killed.] Another young man in Georgia was killed while trying to vote. The NAACP in New York was active and concerned with these things. And we, as members of the theater, were approached by the NAACP and by the Urban League to make ourselves involved, to help them raise funds, to help them spread the word, to take part in the pageants that they put on. So it was sort of a natural progression. And to take part in those pageants was not just to do something in the cause of liberation, freedom for black folks. You'd be on the stage with Paul Robeson or Lena Horne or Canada Lee or some of the others, and of course, that alone was sufficient to get us involved. But the theaters from which we came were dedicated in their own way to trying to improve the lot of the actors, and that has a civil rights aspect to it.

So coming into the theater was the result, we thought, of struggle, and when we got in, we had to do something about all those lynchings that were taking place, particularly in the South. There was no federal anti–lynching law, and Paul Robeson was active in trying to get one. Whenever there was a crime in the South, if a Willie McGee was in trouble or a Rosalee Ingram and her sons in Florida or the Martinsville Seven being accused of rape or a Harry T. Moore (somebody put a bomb in his room at Christmastime), we were a part of that reservoir of workers and actors who would spring into action. It was just a part of being in the theatrical community as far as I was concerned. It took no persuading. It took no deciding, "I must do this." It was being done, and I just participated in it.

APPENDIX

[The following is a statement published by the Briggs-DeLaine-Pearson Foundation, and is reprinted with permission.]

The Briggs-DeLaine-Pearson Foundation

Overview. Briggs-DeLaine-Pearson Foundation (BDPF) is a 501(c)(3) public charity, a nonprofit volunteer organization in the economically distressed, rural town of Summerton in Clarendon County, South Carolina. Since 2002, it has targeted the Clarendon County School District One community as its primary service area.

District One includes approximately one-third of the county, including Summerton. BDPF's entire service community is all of Clarendon County and the immediately surrounding areas.

Our Mission and Vision. BDPF was originally founded in 1993 with the simple goals of:

Memorializing the people responsible for the *Briggs v. Elliott* lawsuit, and housing *Briggs* memorabilia in a community center.

The two missions of BDPF are:

1. To perpetuate the legacy of the *Briggs v. Elliott* lawsuit of making positive community changes by facilitating the educational, social, and physical well-being of all members of the community.

2. To honor and memorialize the people whose courage and sacrifices were responsible for *Briggs v. Elliott* by stressing educational achievement, knowledge of local history and responsible citizenship.

The Foundation's vision is of a thriving community that:

a. provides opportunities for each individual to make positive contributions for the common good, and

b. recognizes the historical contributions of all its citizens.

This vision is based on a philosophy that—if supplied with appropriate opportunities, resources, and encouragement—all people of the community can realize their full potential.

Our objectives are:

1. To foster the creation of programs and partnerships that address educational, social and medical needs of people in the Clarendon County area.
2. To encourage personal and community development.
3. To inspire a sense of pride in local history.
4. To develop a permanent center to house BDPF programs, BDPF offices, a new community center, and *Briggs v. Elliott* artifacts.

Our Enrichment/Tutorial Program serves more than forty District One children, the number being limited only by the condition and size of our facility. Available support includes academic assistance with language arts, social studies and mathematics. Enrichment activities encourage students to apply previously acquired knowledge to new situations, as well as to develop skills of observation, interpretation, and critical thinking. This program is currently supported by individual donors and by funds from State Street Global Philanthropy Fund.

A new BDPF program, **Parents as Partners in Education**, has the aim of creating a powerful constituency of families that will foster improvement in literacy and educational achievement of District One's school children. Start-up funds have come from the Verizon Literacy Foundation. Additional funding is currently being sought.

Our Healthy Choices/Healthy Lifestyles Program seeks to promote healthy lifestyles and reduce risky behaviors by cultivating youth as good health advocates. It also engages a group of highly "at risk" children in focused and individualized intervention activities. This program is supported by funds from Clarendon County Turning Point.

To help trigger economic development in the targeted area, BDPF conceived the idea of a Sewing Cooperative. Although a submitted grant proposal was not funded, a partnership with the Rural Development Office of the South Carolina U.S. Department of Agriculture has developed.

Collaborative efforts have resulted in the creation of an incorporated entity named Sew What, Inc. Funds are being sought to help cooperative members purchase equipment and materials.

Our Summer Science Camp for middle school students will be offered again in Summer 2006 at the District One Middle School. This initiative is a partnership between BDPF and District One. It is supported by individual donations and in-kind donations from the school district.

Via membership in NAEIR, we continue to supply goods to Clarendon County public schools. To date, the market value of goods delivered (classroom supplies, educational materials, etc.) is in excess of $70,000.00 This initiative is supported by individual donations.

With money from donations and grants, we sponsor educational trips for groups of District One students. In partnership with Randolph Middle School (Charlotte, NC), BDPF is sponsoring a select group of District One eighth grade students on a four-day educational historic Civil Rights tour. Partial funding for the trip was obtained from the Knight Foundation. At least three additional day trips to historic/educational sites in South Carolina will be arranged for other groups of District One students (State Street Global Philanthropy Fund).

We are engaged in a Capital Building Campaign to raise funds for a permanent BDPF Center. Unfortunately, legal, financial, and logistic problems prevent us from sharing school facilities, and Summerton—like most small towns—has no suitable rental properties. The new BDPF center will be placed on property already owned by BDPF. When we move from our present inadequate, cramped, and borrowed quarters, the new location will be able to accommodate a new community center, in addition to its offices, other programs, and *Briggs v. Elliott* artifacts.

BDP Foundation
P.O. Box 155
Summerton, SC 29148

Briggs-DeLaine-Pearson Foundation
1578 Gov. Richardson Road
Summerton, SC 29148
803.485.2196

www.bdpfoundation.org

[The following is a statement published by the Aesthetic Realism Foundation, and is reprinted with permission.]

Aesthetic Realism Foundation
Mission Statement & Description

The purpose of the not-for-profit Aesthetic Realism Foundation is to meet the urgent need for people throughout America and the world to see each other and reality fairly. The means to that fairness is Aesthetic Realism, the philosophy founded in 1941 by Eli Siegel, American poet, critic, and educator—which is based on the following principles, stated by Mr. Siegel:

1. The deepest desire of every person is to like the world on an honest or accurate basis.

2. The greatest danger for a person is to have contempt for the world and what is in it. Contempt can be defined as the lessening of what is different from oneself as a means of self-increase as one sees it.

3. All beauty is a making one of opposites, and the making one of opposites is what we are going after in ourselves.

The Foundation is dedicated to the understanding of, and greater respect for, people, art, and reality.

Aesthetic Realism explains that the largest fight in every person is between liking the world on an honest basis and having contempt for the world. There is no more important contribution to human thought than Eli Siegel's identification of contempt as the source of all unkindness between people, including economic injustice, racism, war. And the means to change contempt is the aesthetic criticism of self: Aesthetic Realism is the study of how we want to put together the opposites that are one in art—including care for ourselves and justice to the world.

At the Foundation

At once widely cultural and of the most practical personal value, Aesthetic Realism is education of a new kind, taught by a faculty of Consultants and Associates. Classes offered on a semester basis include: The Aesthetic Realism Explanation of Poetry; Anthropology Is about You and Everyone; The Opposites in Music; The Art of Drawing: Surface and Depth; Acting, Life, and the Opposites. There are monthly workshops: Aesthetic Realism and Marriage; Learning to Like the World, a class for young people between the ages of five and twelve; and Critical Inquiry: A Workshop in the Visual Arts.

The Aesthetic Realism Teaching Method Workshop is a class for educators, and for over thirty years this method, used by public school teachers, has enabled students at every level to learn with new enthusiasm and ease.

Public Seminars and Events

On the first Thursday of every month the Foundation's distinguished faculty of Consultants and Associates presents public seminars. Representative subjects include: "Real Communication in Marriage—How Can We Have It?"; "What's the Difference between Wowing People & Liking Yourself?"; "Kindness: Is It Strong?"; "The Aesthetic Realism Teaching Method Succeeds: Knowledge Wins, Prejudice Loses!"

Saturday Evening Public Presentations

These feature dramatic readings of some of the great lectures on literature, ethics, economics, history, everyday life, and art given by Eli Siegel. There are reenactments of Aesthetic Realism lessons he taught, upon which Aesthetic Realism consultations today are based. And there are groundbreaking talks by artists and scholars in many fields—including jazz, architecture, photography, film—on this new way of seeing the arts, sciences—and reality itself.

Aesthetic Realism Consultations

In consultations, a person's individual life questions are understood and explained, through the principles of Aesthetic Realism. People find that the matters which confuse them most are made sense of at last, with cultural width, immediacy, and satisfying logic. Consultations may be had in person at the Foundation or via telephone throughout America and abroad.

The Aesthetic Realism Theatre Company

Pioneering dramatic and musical presentations take place at the Foundation, and elsewhere as part of the Foundation's Outreach Program. These productions—a new dramatic form with performance and comment—include "Shakespeare's *A Midsummer Night's Dream*; or, Earthy Whirl," by Eli Siegel; "American Ethics, American Song"; "Symmetry & Fury—in Sheridan, Handel, & Our Lives!"; and more. [www.aestheticrealismtheatreco.org]

The Terrain Gallery

The Terrain is the first gallery to show the inextricable relation between the technique of art and people's lives. Since its opening in 1955 in New York City, the Terrain has presented exhibitions of contemporary paintings, prints, drawings, and photographs, with comment based on Eli Siegel's now historic Fifteen Questions, "Is Beauty the Making One of Opposites?" Among the artists exhibiting have been Will Barnet, Chaim Koppelman, Robert Blackburn, Ad Reinhardt, Nell Blaine, Andre Kertesz, William King, Red Grooms, Isabel Bishop, Rolph Scarlett.

Speakers Bureau & Outreach Programs

The Foundation provides speakers on a wide range of subjects, from education to love; jazz to parenting; architecture and film to the combating of prejudice. Its very successful Outreach Programs include presentations and workshops for senior citizens in both English and Spanish, and for young people at community centers, schools, and libraries throughout the New York metropolitan area and beyond, as well as anti-prejudice workshops for people of all ages.

It is also possible to study Aesthetic Realism anywhere in the world through the Foundation's Website and Online Library. These are rich with articles; poetry; works on literature, philosophy, the social sciences, the arts—all in relation to life as people live it. The biweekly international periodical *The Right of Aesthetic Realism to Be Known* [TRO] features commentaries by Ellen Reiss on immediate life, world happenings, economics, the arts. In TRO, people can study landmark works by Eli Siegel, and writings by Consultants and Associates.

Professional classes for Aesthetic Realism Consultants and for Associates studying to teach Aesthetic Realism are conducted by Ms. Reiss, who was appointed Class Chairman by Eli Siegel.

The effect of the Aesthetic Realism education on people's lives is tremendously beneficial, and thrilling. Men, women, and young persons learn to see other people, the world, and themselves more exactly—with honest respect and therefore much more pleasure. They like the world and themselves more, feel freer, are more expressed, kinder, deeper, keener, and happier. Aesthetic Realism is education urgently needed by America and the world.

Note: The following is reprinted from the Aesthetic Realism Foundation website.

Eli Siegel Day, 2002. To honor the centenary of the birth of Eli Siegel, Congressman Elijah E. Cummings, Chair of the Congressional Black Caucus, entered a Tribute to him in the U.S. Congressional Record. August 16, 2002, was proclaimed "Eli Siegel Day" by Governor Glendening of Maryland and Mayor Martin O'Malley of Baltimore, the city in which Mr. Siegel grew up and where his thought and writing began. On that day, Baltimore's Department of Recreation and Parks and the Aesthetic Realism Foundation co-sponsored the dedication of the Eli Siegel Memorial in Druid Hill Park, near his early home. As part of the ceremony, men and women noted in diverse fields spoke about the importance of Mr. Siegel's work for education, the arts, economics, and people's lives— including the answer to racism which it provides.

(left to right) Allan Michael, Monique Michael, Dr. Jaime Torres, Dr. Arnold Perey, speak about the answer to racism on Eli Siegel Day (8-16-02) in Baltimore, Maryland (Photo Credit: Vincent DiPietro)

Aesthetic Realism Foundation
141 Greene Street
New York, NY 10012
(212) 777-4490

www.aestheticrealism.org

BIOGRAPHICAL NOTES

Ossie Davis (1917–2005), actor, director, writer, producer, and civil rights activist, was born in Cogdell, Georgia. He graduated from Howard University in 1938. His acting career began the following year, with the Rose McClendon Players in Harlem. In 1946, he made his Broadway debut in *Jeb*, where he also met actress Ruby Dee. They were married in 1948 and had three children. His Broadway credits include *Anna Lucasta, The Wisteria Trees, Green Pastures, Jamaica, Ballad for Bimshire, A Raisin in the Sun, The Zulu and the Zayda, I'm Not Rappaport.* In 1950 he made his film debut in *No Way Out*, which starred Sidney Poitier.

In 1961, Ossie Davis wrote and starred in the critically acclaimed Broadway production *Purlie Victorious.*

Mr. Davis was an activist for civil rights and social justice all his life. He worked with Dr. Martin Luther King, Jr. in the 1960s and was a tireless fundraiser for the Freedom Riders. The high respect in which he was held, and his voice as a spokesperson for the African American community, can be seen in the fact that he gave eulogies at the funerals of both Dr. Martin Luther King, Jr. and Malcolm X.

He wrote and directed many films, including *Cotton Comes to Harlem* and *Countdown at Kusini*, which he co-produced with Ruby Dee. His film credits include *Dr. Doolittle, Get on the Bus* and *I'm Not Rappaport*, and his extensive television credits include *Bonanza; Car 54, Where Are You?; N.Y.P.D.* His writings include fiction, drama, speeches, and poetry.

Mr. Davis was inducted into the Theater Hall of Fame in 1994, and his many awards and honors include the Hall of Fame Award for Outstanding Artistic Achievement in 1989, U.S. National Medal for the Arts in 1995, the New York Urban League Frederick Douglass Award, NAACP Image Award, and the Screen Actor's Guild Lifetime Achievement Award in 2001. Ossie Davis and Ruby Dee were named to the NAACP Image Awards Hall of Fame in 1989. In 2004, they were recipients of the Kennedy Center Honors. Mr. Davis died on February 5, 2005.

In 2007, the dual autobiography, *With Ossie & Ruby—In This Life Together*, won a Grammy Award for Best Spoken Word Recording Category.

A collection of selected speeches and writings by Ossie Davis, *Life Lit by Some Large Vision* (Atria Books), was published in 2007 with editorial notes and foreword by Ruby Dee.

Alice Bernstein is an Aesthetic Realism Associate and journalist whose articles and regular column, "Alice Bernstein & Friends," appear in newspapers nationwide. She began her study of Aesthetic Realism with its founder, Eli Siegel, and continues today in professional classes taught by Class Chairman Ellen Reiss.

Congressman Elijah Cummings (D-MD), former Chair of the Congressional Black Caucus, described Mrs. Bernstein as having "contributed significantly to promoting an increased understanding between races in this country." As a journalist she has interviewed artists, lawyers, labor leaders, judges, educators, and elected officials.

In 2005, she received the first of several grants from philanthropists and nonprofit foundations for an oral history project and documentary on "The Force of Ethics in the Struggle for Civil Rights." This project includes interviews with unsung heroes around the country, and is sponsored by the Alliance of Ethics & Art, a not-for-profit corporation. As 2007, began, Mrs. Bernstein had conducted interviews with over 100 men and women, which were videotaped by photographer and cameraman David Bernstein, who is her husband.

About her work, State Representative Tyrone Brooks of Georgia writes, "I am grateful for what Alice Bernstein is doing to preserve our history and bring it to the forefront so that it captures the attention of young people."

She is editor and co-author of *Aesthetic Realism and the Answer to Racism* (Orange Angle Press, 2004), and a contributing writer for *African American National Biography*, edited by Henry Louis Gates, Jr. and Evelyn Brooks Higginbotham (Oxford University Press, forthcoming, 2008).